Natural Energy Defense

Learn to Engage Your Inner Energy Defenses for Health, Happincss and Ease

by

Shari Stevens

Natural Energy Defense by Shari Stevens. Published by Pink Stone Press Iowa City, Iowa 52245

www.pinkstonepress.com

© 2021 Shari Stevens

All rights reserved. No portion of this book may be reproduced in any form without permission from the publisher, except as permitted by U.S. copyright law.

Disclaimer

The information contained in this book, including ideas, suggestions, techniques, meditations, and other materials, is provided to you for educational purposes only.

Shari Stevens does not provide medical diagnosis, or consultations related to health, medical, or psychiatric issues. Natural Energy Defense should be used as a complement to professional medical and psychiatric care. Shari Stevens is not a medical doctor or other licensed health care professional, and cannot and will not provide you with any kind of medical care, treatment, or diagnosis in relation to physical, mental or emotional health. When incorporating meditation and guided imagery into your daily routine as a personal relaxation and stress relief practice, you should speak with your medical professional. If you have or suspect that you have a medical problem, please promptly contact your health care provider to seek professional medical attention. Using the exercises in this book is not a substitute for medical or psychological treatment from licensed and registered healthcare professionals. This book and its exercises are meant to be used as a compliment to whatever protocol you may already be on.

The meditations contained in this book can bring up personal and or challenging emotions about intimate topics and issues, including deep-seated trauma. It is the responsibility of the reader to seek therapeutic, psychiatric or medical care when needed.

Any information, stories, examples, or testimonials presented in this book do not constitute a warranty, guarantee, or prediction regarding the outcome for any particular person.

To the maximum extent permitted by law, Shari Stevens disclaims liability for any damages, including, without limitation, direct or indirect, special, incidental, compensatory, exemplary or consequential damages, losses or expenses. By purchasing this book, you agree to fully release, indemnify, and hold harmless,

Shari Stevens, and others associated with Shari Stevens, from any claim or liability whatsoever, including, without limitation, direct or indirect, special, incidental, compensatory, exemplary or consequential damages, losses or expenses.

If any court of law rules that any part of this indemnity, release or disclaimer is invalid, the indemnity, release or disclaimer stands as if those parts were struck out. This book contains copyrighted material (all rights reserved). You may not disseminate, modify, copy, in whole or in part, such copyrighted material unless specifically permitted to do so by Shari Stevens.

By reading this book, you agree to all of the above.

Table of Contents

Your Natural Energy Defenses

You have the right and the ability to defend yourself energetically in all circumstances, at all times and in powerful and effective ways. If you don't know how to do that, and you are unsure about your right to do that, this book is for you. The exercises provided in this book make up a system of learning, transformation and growth that engage and enhance your natural ability to allow the energy within your system to create a system of protection.

These energy defenses work very much like your immune system. Like your immune system, your natural energy defenses are always learning new ways to bring you balance and wellness. They are fueled by love and informed by wisdom. This love energy naturally repels lower energies like aggression, hatred or oppression or other energies like depression or fear. It does not mean you should take foolish risks or that you are magically immune from life's challenges. It does mean that you are deeply connected to your intuition, wisdom and loving protection that will keep you out of sync with the thoughts, beliefs, emotions and ways of being that want to drag you down.

The exercises in this book help you see, feel and experience connections between your inner wisdom and your natural energy defenses. In this way, your ability to be energetically protected and balanced grows and changes based on knowings, intuitive information and energy from your highest source of goodness and your wealth of inner wisdom along with a boundless flow of love.

While some may doubt that they have any inner wisdom at all, I believe they do. I believe that we all have access to, the right to and the power to learn from within. The ability to access this inner strength is a learnable skill. If you are willing to put in the time and the focus, these exercises will bring more safety, strength and more groundedness to your inner being. These exercises will change the way you use your energy. Those changes on the inside will help you make positive changes in your outer world. Your energetic defense is your creation. You create and augment these defenses through your time, attention, intention and willingness to change and grow.

The majority of this book contains exercises that will help you discover your ability to stand your ground energetically and to use that ability in positive ways. Most of the exercises will follow this format:

1. Accessing information from your inner wisdom;
2. Detaching from distressing emotions, traumas, wounds or beliefs that conflict with your inner wisdom, and;
3. Opening to empowerment that is guided by your inner wisdom.

Each exercise will use a type of guided meditation that connects you to the highest and best information that is tailored for you as an individual. I believe that your inner wisdom knows how to best prepare you for your next adventures in life. This inner wisdom knows who you are and the potentials of who you may become. It knows where you need to learn and grow in order to become the best you. This best version of you has the safety, security and confidence to help you grow your gifts and bring them to the world. Being able to defend yourself energetically with integrity, honor and love is a powerful way to give goodness to the world.

Your natural energy defense system is a kind of mindset that is meant to support and augment the body's own healing system. It is based on the idea that what your conscious mind focuses on creates beliefs within your subconscious that work with your body-mind connection. In the exercises below, we will use guided meditation, also known as guided imagery, to help you apply that focus. Guided imagery uses internal mechanisms that are activated by creating mental images, paired with emotion to jumpstart the placebo effect or the mind-body connection. It has been proven time and again that what you focus on, in a highly focused state, will become real to the unconscious mind and will have great impacts in the real world.

Research has found that imagery and meditation on strengthening exercises increased strength. In a 2004 study, one group of subjects did finger exercises meant to increase strength five days a week for 12 weeks. The second group did guided imagery of those exercises as often for the same time frame. The control group did nothing. At the end of the study, it was found that the first group increased strength by 53%. The second, imagery only, group increased strength by 35% and the control group did not change. Another study of individuals in wrist casts who imagined strengthening exercises were twice as strong as those who did not use imagery. Your conscious awareness follows your unconscious reality. Change the unconscious reality, and the experience of your life will change too.

The Energetic Defense system is different from guided imagery alone in a couple of ways. First, it works with and engages our very real energy system which is the foundation of our health and balance. Second, the exercises in this book help and teach you how to connect with and learn from your own inner wisdom. My inner wisdom was the source of the two "visions" I shared above, along with all of the other deep and meaningful learning I have experienced from within. Perhaps you too have had flashes of intuitive insight, knowings or other connections to your inner wisdom.

The Energetic Defense system creates a solid connection between that wisdom and the parts of your energy system that are meant to support, protect and heal you. If you feel as if your inner protection has let you down in the past, this system helps your inner protection to learn, grow, and do more for you. The exercises included in this book create a structure that allows your conscious mind to relax and get out of the way of your energy defenses while giving those defenses access to deeper truths than our conscious mind might hold. The result is deeper feelings of safety paired with the transformation that can only be brought by your inner wisdom.

The Author's Story

Hello, my name is Shari Stevens. I'm a healer with 20 years of experience working daily with clients who come to me with a broad spectrum of pains, dysfunctions and life issues. Over time, I have learned a great deal about what helps people heal and what does not. I have come to believe that it all starts with safety. You can't heal physically until you can relax because a person caught in fight or flight can't access their healing mechanisms. You can't heal emotionally if all of your attention is on the thing or things you are fearing or fighting. You can't heal spiritually if you are disconnected from the flow of wellbeing that helps to create safety. The purpose of this book is to help you connect with, learn about and experience your own inner energy defenses. It is these inner energetic defenses that allow us to relax, turn our attention to the good, and reconnect to our birthright of wellbeing. I want to recount to you the journey that I took with energy healing so that you can understand my perspective on healing and find some new ideas about your own growth and transformation.

In the Beginning . . .

Ha! There is no beginning to my journey as a healer. I have always been intuitive, always an empath, or as they would have said back in the day, "sensitive." Then, it was said with a sad shake of the head, but now, of course, we see nuances in this way of experiencing the world.

But perhaps one beginning to this journey may have been on an evening in 1967.

I had a headache. It was a big thing for a little kid. I was five. As my mother was reaching for the aspirin, I said to her, "Can't you feel it?"

"Feel what?" she asked.

"My head," putting my hands on my temples.

She smiled. "No," she said.

I took her hand and put it on my head. "There, can you feel it there?" I asked.

She shook her head with the kind of amusement reserved for kids being cute, "No, I can't feel it."

"Why not?" I demanded. I could feel her confusion in trying to form an answer.

"People don't feel other people's pain," she finally said.

Now I was confused. That seemed just wrong. It was then that I began to see that I experienced the world differently than others.

Spin forward twenty plus years. In the meantime, I grew into an adult, went to college and law school, got a job as a public defender doing appellate work and found myself working in a 1950's era office building across from the State Capitol building in Des Moines, Iowa. Picture this, one whole floor of open concept, a sea of cubicles, ancient linoleum on the floor and fluorescent lighting above. Drill down to the northeast corner and picture me, in my cubicle, working through lunch. The place is deserted and quiet. It's just me and one other lawyer, working through lunch. Suddenly I hear from the other lawyer, I'll call her Ann, "Shari, Shari, Shari, come quick! You've got to take me to the hospital. Something is wrong with my leg!" I ran over there, where she was gripping her leg in anguish.

"What's wrong?" I ask.

"It hurts!" she responds. "I don't know if I can move it."

Now, what comes next comes from I don't know where. Somehow I just knew that I had to put my hands on her leg and project love to it. So I said, "Can I just do something?"

And for some reason, she said, "Okay."

I sat down in a chair next to her, placed my hands on the place on her thigh that she had been gripping and opened my heart. I imagined that love was flowing from my heart to my hands and to her leg. After about 30 seconds or more, definitely less than a minute, I looked at her. She said with amazement, "It's better." We looked at each other, kind of shrugged, and I asked, "Do you still need to go to the hospital?"

"No," she said. "It doesn't hurt anymore."

"Okay," I said, and I returned to my office and went back to work.

Looking back, I now see several oddities about this incident, above and beyond the healing. First and foremost, other than Jesus, I had never heard of anyone even trying to do a thing like that. The idea came from nowhere. Second, I am amazed that I decided to act on this. To my mind at the time, it was an outlandish idea. Third, I'm amazed that Ann readily agreed! And finally, we both just went on with our business as if nothing happened.

Spin forward about one month. Again, Ann and I are the only ones working through lunch. Again, Ann's leg begins to hurt, and she calls to me over the cubicle dividers, "Oh no! My leg is hurting again!" This time, Ann comes to my cubicle and sits in the chair next to the door. I ask, "Do you want me to do that thing again?" and she nods and says, "Yes."

So, I do the same thing. I get up from my desk, go over to her and put my hands on her leg. I open my heart, intending love and it just seems to go through my hands. This time, we look at each other and laugh, but we don't discuss it. We just shrug. Maybe neither of us had the right vocabulary to even talk about this unusual thing we had experienced. I know I couldn't have described what happened, other than it had something to do with love.

I eventually moved on from that job to one downtown and then to another town. But about eight years later, I met up with Ann at a conference. After a happy greeting, she turned to me and said, "You know that thing that happened with my leg?" Of course, I knew exactly what she was talking about. "The pain never came back," she said. "Wow, that's great. I'm glad." I replied. Again, we just shrugged and moved on.

Sometime around the leg love incident, I took up meditation. I had a stressful job, my personal life seemed chaotic, and I was anxious. I wanted to feel calm, happy, safe. My daily meditation was to create a personal "safe place" in my imagination. I could "go there" and just rest. A funny thing happened, though. Sometimes when I really got into it, I would have a kind of rolling warmth come up from my feet. It would go up my legs and kind of fill my body. It left me feeling like I was floating about three inches above where I was laying down. It felt really good. I liked it. What I didn't like was the reaction I would get when I asked people what that was. I would try to describe it to my friends and say, "Do you know what that is?" Always, I would get a blank look with the answer, "No." No one knew. Oh well. I moved on.

About two years after I started meditating, a friend came to me with great excitement. "Shari, you have to try this thing," she said.

"What thing?" I asked.

"There's this thing that I did today, and you have to try it!"

My eyes narrow as I look at her. "Uhhhh, what? What is it?"

She just laughed and said, "I don't know what it is, but you will love it. I went for an appointment with this lady, and she did some kind of energy thing, and I know that you should try it, and you'll like it!"

I looked at my friend with deep skepticism. Even though this is after the leg love incident, after the floaty meditation experiences, I don't connect the dot, but I do take my friend's advice. What the heck, I thought. I'm up for something different.

So the following week, I found myself in an ordinary office building near downtown Des Moines, filling out an intake sheet as if I was going to meet with a doctor. But the woman I was meeting with was no doctor. She had the professionalism of a healthcare professional, but she was dressed in business casual and showed me into a room that contained a massage table rather than an exam table. Her name was Kathy Reardon, and in her kind and gentle way, she changed my whole understanding of how the world works.

She told me that she was going to do a therapy called Healing Touch. It was energy healing, and I was to lay down on the massage table, fully clothed, of course, and just relax. She would do a little self-preparation and then begin with her hands on my feet. As she went on, she would put her hands on or over areas of my body. She said that I should find it very relaxing.

So, I climbed up on the massage table, closed my eyes and tried to relax. I had no idea what I was doing there. Then she put her hands on my feet, and I knew. I knew! This was the same feeling I got from deep meditation. Finally, an answer! As she went on, however, I understood that the warm feeling, the experience of an undefinable movement of something going through my body was much, much stronger than I could do with my daily meditation. Then, she put her hands over my throat. I felt like I was drinking something. Something I had been thirsty for my whole life. Holy cow! This was unbelievable. I was hooked.

Unfortunately, I had only a handful of sessions with Kathy. I was moving from Des Moines to Iowa City. But Kathy came through with a referral to another Healing Touch practitioner, this one in a city about 30 minutes from where I was moving. At the time, I thought I was merely receiving healing sessions to combat the stress in my life. I had plenty of it. I thought the move would help my unhappiness at work, but the truth was, I was burned out. I was also having a difficult time meeting new friends in a new city. I had plenty of reasons to seek healing, but in truth, I was experiencing an initiation into the world of healing.

My new healer, Janny Adkins, was sharing a whole different world with me. In this world, a normal person could communicate clearly with their intuition. In this world, it was normal to feel and experience energies. It was normal to use love as a healing force. In this world, spiritual connection and daily life are tightly interwoven so that intuition, healing, and transformation belong inside the meditation room and out. The weave of spirit and daily life could and did breathe life into everything from banishing pain to finding a parking spot. I found that changing my perspective to seeing the energy in things, both good and bad, helped me find meaning, even in an unhappy time of my life. Janny did one more thing for me. She pushed, and pushed and pushed on me until I agreed to learn Reiki.

So there I am, minding my own business, sitting in a darkened room with about a dozen other people, waiting to learn Reiki. I had experienced Reiki before. Janny had tried it out on me several times. As I waited for the class to begin, I had no great expectations. I thought it might be nice to take a little two-day course that would teach me more about this energy thing. And then in walks Laurelle, the Reiki Master Teacher. In her quiet, serene way, she began to talk about Reiki and life force energy and intuition and even spirit guides as if they were as real as the chair she was sitting on. Then she did an exercise called an attunement which made it possible for us to be able to do Reiki. The attunement was pretty simple, just sitting in a circle with Laurelle moving from student to student, moving our hands around, sometimes patting us, sometimes blowing on us, and sometimes just putting her hands on our shoulders.

As usual, I could feel the flow of energy. This was not new to me. What was new was being able to do something with it. I had instructions, a protocol, a way of understanding what I was doing and some idea, at least, about what to do with the energy. Laurelle had us practice on ourselves and on each other. The true revelation was in the feedback from my practice buddies. They told me that they could feel the Reiki energy from my hands and that it made them feel better. I decided then and there to quit my job as a lawyer and start up a whole new life as a healer.

For the previous two years, I had been telling my friends that I wanted a different job. "It has to be something that helps people," I would say. "But I don't want to listen to people's problems," I would add. "It doesn't have to make as much as a lawyer, but I want a comfortable living without a mountain of paperwork and something that has a clear beginning, middle and end and doesn't drag on and on for months." I knew I didn't want to be a therapist or social worker or work in a different legal area. What I really wanted was to free myself from my desk, liberate myself from the combat zone called the courtroom and forever release the painful stories of the wretched things that people do to each other.

I would like to say that I courageously handed in my two-week notice that next Monday, but this is not true. No, I tried to ride the fence. I knew I could never make a comfortable living doing Reiki alone. But what about massage school, I thought. I could do both Reiki and massage. Massage school was just a six-month program. What if I get a six month leave of absence and do Reiki and massage on the side? The powers that be said no way. In this, I mean both the higher ups in the Public Defender's Office and my own personal higher power. Apparently, if I was going to do this thing, it was all or nothing. So, I put on my big girl panties and did it.

Unfortunately, learning a new craft and starting my own business was much harder than I expected. I struggled, a lot at first. As an aside, I think that if I have a tombstone, it should read, "She foolishly thought it would be easy, but she got it done in the end." It wasn't until much later, when I learned Thetahealing®, that I could transform my financial security. However, during the infancy of my massage and Reiki business, I was flooded with creative energy. Despite the finances, I was extremely happy, doing daily Reiki on myself, learning to put Reiki into everything from painting a room to helping found an arts organization or doing my own creative projects. It was fun, filled with parties, dancing and building new things. I attribute the fun, the joy and the creativity to my work with Reiki along with the awesomeness of my friends. I was also doing a great deal of experimentation with Reiki. This was partly due to my Reiki Master training. One part of the master training includes meditations to help focus the mind and intensify the Reiki energy. I would do the meditation and ask a question. Often the answer I received came in a sort of vision that I think must be very much like shamanic journeying. I want to share two of these visions, as they have created cornerstones for my approach to energy healing.

One of the visions had to do with truth. I did the Reiki meditation, which must have put me into a deep trance state. Then, I asked the question, "What is truth?" I meant this in the connotation of religious truth. In other words, I was asking what I should know about the truth espoused by all of the world's religions. For some time, all I could see in my mind's eye was blackness, but then it took on the feeling or knowing or connotation of space. But this space had no stars. Then, my attention caught on a huge, bright diamond shape. This diamond was spinning. It felt like an enormous diamond that was spinning in infinity. It was as if, as I approached the diamond, I too had become huge because I reached out my hands and stopped the spinning of the diamond. I could see into one of the facets as if it was a window. As I looked down through my facet window, I saw an entire world of one of the religions. It was as if I could see people, living the truth of that religion, and it was true, it did work and their system created a complete truth that was real. Then, I released the diamond, and it began to spin again. Once more, I stopped the spin and looked into another facet and saw another group of people, living a completely different truth. As I looked into different facets, I felt a deep knowing that each belief system was true in a human sense, but that no human system could encompass the greater truth. I left this vision with a deeper and stronger respect for other people's belief systems, even those with no spiritual beliefs at all because they are in fact all true, all deserving of respect and all serving the purpose of soul growth.

In the second vision, I didn't exactly ask a question. Instead, I was praying. I was saying thank you, in a rather smug and self-satisfied way. I was saying, "Thank you, God, for all of this spiritual knowledge. It's so great, and I have learned so much." Again, I was taken into a vision. Immediately, I felt as if I was flying. In my imagination, I saw a beautiful tapestry below me. It was so huge that I thought there was no end to it. It was intricate, with flowers and animals and all kinds of scenes that all seemed to fit together into one whole theme. At one point, I flew down close to it and saw that it was three dimensional, that the intricacies extended downward. Then, I was guided to a corner of the tapestry. While I hovered above, I also saw myself kneeling down, with the tapestry in my hands, and I was plucking at a couple of its threads. Then, I became the me that was plucking at the two or three threads. They seemed so fascinating. They made a kind of sound or vibration as I was plucking them. Suddenly I knew, however, that the tapestry was all of life, all of creation and I was only plucking at a few of its threads. I felt a warm and compassionate presence behind me lean down and whisper into my ear, "This is how much you have learned." And an explosion of joy burst through me, sending me upward, flying upward in happiness. There is no end of things to learn! There is no end to the wonder and the joy and the fulfillment of learning about creation. And all of the unconscious pressure to know it all fell away because I knew for sure that none of us could know more than a handful of threads from that tapestry and that was more than enough.

What I took from these two visions was: first, you need to pick your myth. Find what you believe in and explore its parameters. If your myth is based on love, I believe it will work for you. If you graduate or move to another myth, it too will work for you. In my mind, it's all good. Second, life and creation are beautiful and even if we can't see the overarching themes, they are there. We are all free to explore and learn about this lovely creation that is life without having to make it all make sense. If I don't have the perspective to see how it all fits together into something beautiful, I choose to believe that the beauty is there, but just in the bigger picture. You may see how these themes are reflected in the exercises that follow.

I soon began extending my work with Reiki. I found myself naturally using imagery during my Reiki sessions. I felt drawn to helping my clients picture the energy and work with it while I allowed the Reiki to flow to their energy systems. I understood that I was doing a form of guided imagery with my clients. The problem was, I knew very little about guided imagery, and needed to know more. I was very fortunate to find training from Chuck and Patti Leviton at Synergy Seminars.

Their personal story shows the power of guided imagery as an intervention paired with medical care. When Chuck and Patti met, they were both in their middle years, both divorced, both professionals and both on vacation. He lived in California. She lived in Chicago. Within a few hours together, mutual interest turned into love. But, there was a problem. Patti was carrying a deep burden. She was fighting a malignant brain tumor. Initially, radiation killed the tumor while taking the sight in one eye. When Chuck and Patti met, Patti was in the middle of a course of chemotherapy treatment because the tumor had come back. Despite the illness, despite the distance, within 3 months they were both living in southern California, with Patti working at a different branch at her company. For about nine months, they lived an enchanted love story with everything falling into place. Then came the bombshell. The doctors gave Patti six months to live.

As it would happen, Chuck was a specialist in guided imagery. He taught it as a professor at a nearby college, and he used it as a Licensed Marriage and Family Therapist. Patti agreed to learn guided imagery. Despite several months of daily imagery sessions, the doctors gave Patti a terrible choice: a surgery with a one in a million chance of survival, or certain death within days. She took the surgery and miraculously survived and recovered. Both Patti and Chuck attributed her recovery to the combination of skilled medical care and guided imagery. Patti was certain that she would have died without her inner work using imagery to resolve the mental and emotional stresses that drained her system.

Patti also told us in class that her returned sight was entirely due to her dedicated use of guided imagery after the life-saving surgery. She had lost sight in one eye from her initial treatment using radiation. One morning, she was awakened from sleep by a searing pain in that eye. When she could finally open her eyes after the pain ebbed, her sight was back. Scans showed no cancer, no tumor and no scar tissue. She was healed.

Needless to say, both Patti and Chuck were enthusiastic and skilled teachers. They were also playful and creative in their use of guided imagery. What drew me to their program, though, was their emphasis on love and compassion as components in healing. They saw guided imagery as more than a mechanistic imaging of the healing process. Instead, they taught us how to create a positive relationship between the conscious self and the subconscious. Instead of viewing the inner causes of dysfunction as defects, they saw the connection to the subconscious as a way to learn and access information. Their training left me with the belief that the subconscious often knows more about what is going on in the body, mind and heart, than the conscious self.

What their training did not do for me was teach me how to pair what I knew as an energy healer with my new skills as a guided imagery therapist. This, I had to learn for myself. As an aside, please understand that although I am a certified guided imagery therapist, I am not a psychotherapist, counselor, psychologist or therapist. I do not do counseling. I see myself as a guided imagery coach, specializing in energy healing. My specialty is teaching clients and students how to "talk to" their inner being with stories, images and emotion paired with certain types of energy healing that access inner wisdom, connect to positive life force energy and restore balance, the foundation of health and wellbeing. I had to learn how to do this, both on my own and with the help of other teachers.

Learning about energy healing is an odd affair. Every teacher has their own perspective and their own way of accessing and using positive life force energy. Even within the Reiki community, there is a vast banquet of approaches and nuances. Some lean in the direction of beings of light, fairies and angels. Others follow a more eastern, zen mindset. Still, others focus on a shamanic approach. What I wanted was deeper training in using images and symbols in energy healing. My guided imagery training taught me that images and symbols are the language of the unconscious. I knew from my personal experiences that adding energy healing results in higher efficiency and better outcomes. I was lucky enough to hear about Shelley Hodgen from another bodyworker. Shelley's classes taught me about the importance of grounding and running energy. She used positive images, along with imagery of the chakras and parts of the electromagnetic energy field that surrounds every living person. With each class, as well as my own creative approach to energy and imagery, I was learning more and more about the ins and outs of energy healing for the self and for clients.

It wasn't until I tried Thetahealing® that I understood the broad possibilities available from energy healing. I'm going to begin my comments about Thetahealing® by saying that there is no reason that I can understand that it should work. But it does work. It's goofy but good. In a Thetahealing® session, the practitioner finds the client's unconscious, negative belief through a process called muscle testing. This, I can get my head around. Chiropractors use muscle testing. In the healing process, the practitioner asks for permission to ask the Creator of All Things to change the belief to a positive one. Then the practitioner does a meditation, sending his or her consciousness to this higher power or source energy and makes that request with the added request, "Show me." It is the observation of the energetic change, observed by the practitioner that somehow makes the change real for the client. How could this be? This violates every concept of reality that we hold. Yet, I have found it to be extremely effective. I just plain don't know how it works. Is it a function of entrainment and entanglement? Does it reflect the quantum mechanics notions about superposition and the role of the observer? What do I do, as a rational being, faced with the dilemma of a thing that just shouldn't be? I decided that I simply lack the right information to be able to explain this phenomenon. My experience is that it is powerfully positive and that it helps change people's lives for the better.

Thetahealing® taught me a great deal about the process of energy healing. First of all, I've learned that energy healing can be extremely fast. Secondly, Thetahealing® gave me a deeper understanding of the role of learning as a key to healing. Thirdly, it sweeps away questions like, "Am I worthy?" and replaces them with a focus on process, such as, "Do I know how to, for example, be healthy, release resentments, know what it feels like to be financially secure." What if the dysfunction we see all around us is not because people are bad or broken. What if the cause is because they lack an unconscious understanding that it is possible to, or right to change, be happy or live differently? What if it is merely a process problem? These questions spurred me onward.

My twenty plus years of work as a healer have given me the opportunity to see and understand what people do when they do not feel safe or secure. They get tense, anxious. Sleep is disturbed. They may over function by giving too much, trying too hard or controlling everyone and everything around them. They may give up, become passive and hopeless. They may find some unhealthy benefit in woundedness or helplessness. They may use emotional barriers such as hatred, judgement or belligerence. They might detach from their source of life force energy and become dependent upon the energy of others to sustain them. Or they might disconnect from others as a form of defense. At the physical level, I see areas of muscle and connective tissue congestion or even hardness that very much seems like armor. Or, in some, there are areas of great weakness, as if virtually no life force energy flows there. I see energy depletion and exhaustion due to energy leaks. Some people give their power away. Some people have it taken away. Some people attack each other energetically and others are too vulnerable to attack. All of these dysfunctions are rooted in unhealthy beliefs that create unhealthy intentions and unhealthy actions. These unhealthy beliefs also block any healthy or balanced energy that could actually help the person feel grounded, safe and vital. The solution is to engage one's inner wisdom to grow in knowledge and release the dysfunctions.

I have come to the conclusion that we all have so much to learn. Perhaps that potential is a joyful one. It is my hope that these exercises will help you regain your natural flow and support you in your safety, balance and happiness so that your growth and transformation can happen from a place of security and freedom.

A Few Words About Energy Healing

Energy healing is a wide and deep subject. You do not need to know all of its secrets in order to use energy healing in positive ways. In fact, I think you naturally do so all of the time. When you hurt yourself, you put your hand where it hurts. When you are stressed, you take a deep breath. When you feel overwhelmed, you close your eyes and center yourself. When you want to be renewed, you spend some time in nature, watch a kitten or puppy video, or immerse yourself in artistic creation. You know a loving hug can make it all better. You know someone holding your hand can ease your pain. And many or most of you know how to connect with your inner guiding star.

This inner guidance is a little tricky to talk about. This is mostly because there is no one way to be guided, to feel connected or to simply be with this part of our consciousness. You may be a disbeliever. If so, use your ability to suspend your disbelief. You do so every time you pick up a novel. If you have a well formed system of belief around your inner guidance, tailor your experiences of the following exercises in ways that work with your belief system, but also allow that system to change and grow based on the support of your own inner wisdom. The following exercises are meant to set the stage for you to learn from within, not impose beliefs from without.

The following energy healing "principles" may be helpful in understanding how to approach the exercises in this book:

- You are in control of the experience. If you feel like the imagery experience is somehow wrong or overwhelming, take a break, focus on your breath, and if you need to stop and come back to it another day, or with the support of a counselor or qualified energy healer, do so. This is not a sign of weakness or that you are bad at imagery or meditation. In addition, you have the right to and obligation to say no to anything that does not work for you. It may take some time to learn how to distinguish the difference between your fear or resistance to change and your inner wisdom. When in doubt, stop, ask yourself, "Is this right for me?" and "What should I know about this?" You will always be best off when following your intuition in ways that feel safe and balanced.

- Don't force the imagery. If you can't picture something or the energy is not flowing, you will work against yourself if you try to force it. Energy healing is about cooperation with the positive energies that already exist within and around you. You are simply learning to recognize them and work with them. Just pretend as if you could picture, sense or know. Ask yourself, "If I could picture this, what would it look like?" and go with that.

- Love, compassion and gratitude are high vibrational or high frequency energies. I know this sounds very woo-woo, but just stick with me here. Think about energy from Einstein's point of view. Everything is energy. The laws of mathematics and countless experiments have proven this. The study of life at the subatomic level has led researchers to believe that the way energy vibrates will determine how it is expressed in our 3D life. In the world of energy healing, this covers everything, from whether something is a rock or a flower to whether a person is happy or sad or sick or healthy and everything in between. If you want to see a demonstration of what that might look like, do an internet search on experiments with a Chladni plate, and you will see that when a free moving plate covered with sand is subjected to sound frequency, the sand naturally gravitates to form geometric shapes. As the frequency rises, the shapes become more intricate, complicated, beautiful. They are more ordered and structured. Imagine that your emotions and beliefs could become more intricate and beautiful, less chaotic and more ordered, less scary and more structured. Imagine that the structure of your physical being could be supported by energies that facilitate the highest order, structure and health for you. Imagine too that these energies are the energies of unconditional love, paired with your own inner wisdom. And finally, imagine that these energies are in you, as they blossom into your awareness, your being falls into natural sync with them and falls out of sync with the stuff you don't want. This leaves you with more freedom, joy and inspiration. I believe that the goal of all of this is not to get good stuff or repel bad stuff, but to learn and grow as a being.

- Your beliefs rule your experience. It goes like this: your beliefs create your perceptions, your perceptions create your thoughts, your thoughts create your emotions, your emotions influence your choices, your choices determine your actions and your actions create your life. Energy healers believe that beliefs, perceptions, thoughts, emotions are all energies. Raise the vibration or frequency of your beliefs to something that aligns with your inner wisdom and the rest will follow.

- You are always syncing and unsyncing with energies. You control and manage this with your thoughts, intentions and focus. And, when your focus and intention are aligned with other energies, the sync happens naturally, without effort. Neuroscientists have now found that the brains of two people in conversation sync up. The experiments show that the neurological activity of the speaker and listener takes place at the same time in the same way. They call it neural coupling. Interestingly, this neural coupling does not occur with two people who disagree. This is a great metaphor for the process of energy healing. It is a communication of sorts that allows for greater understanding and a richer experience.

- All of creation is balanced in favor of love and goodness, and it is natural to be attracted by what is good, beautiful, True, etc. While it is possible to hold beliefs such as hate is love or cruelty is kindness, and these beliefs may cloud a person's perception, the deeper consciousness of the person is still drawn to the good. It is the journey of traveling to your own sense of what is good that creates your perception of yourself, your life and what it means to be a being within creation.

- Emotions and ways of being such as courage, diligence, integrity or strength can be created without pain or deprivation.

- Intuition can be developed and honed and is essential to anyone seeking empowerment through love and goodness.

- All healing is self healing, and every person is a self healer. That means that if you want health and balance, you must change the way you use or experience energy. That shift happens when you change the way you think, believe or perceive life or yourself or some other deep aspect of life. This kind of change is a shift in your way of being, and that can only come from within.

- The only person you can change is yourself. You cannot decide for another person. This is a function of free will. If you try to force healing or goodness on another person, it will violate their free will and will not bring the good you seek.

- Healing and growth happen when a person is ready. Don't try to force yourself or anyone else to heal, grow or change. If a person is not ready, it will just not work, even if they desire change. Those who are not ready to change can make an intention to receive help in getting ready to change or learn what is necessary in order for change to happen.

- A person can be spiritual without being religious, and it is that spirituality which turns our attention to something bigger or more profound than ourselves that can transform our perspectives so that all of life, even the most difficult parts, are a part of a bigger whole that is good, doable and safe.

- One large aspect of healing is learning at an unconscious level. As the unconscious parts of ourselves adopt new beliefs, perspectives and ways of being, our conscious experience can become more secure, fulfilling and joyful.

How to Use this Book

This book contains guided meditation exercises. You may choose to read and follow the exercises with your imagination as you read along, or you may make an audio recording of the exercises and visualize them as you listen to the playback, or you can have a friend read them aloud as you follow the imagery. Each exercise includes a grounding meditation and an imagery meditation. These must be done together. The purpose of the grounding meditation is to focus and slow your mind's activity. I present the grounding meditation separate from the imagery meditation in order to help your mind sustain the focus necessary to get the most out of the imagery experience. By coming back to normal, waking consciousness even for a moment or two after the grounding exercise, your mind gets the rest it needs to follow the entirety of the following imagery meditation.

I strongly urge you to do these exercises in the order presented. The learning and imagined experience of each will prepare you for the next exercise. I also suggest that you take some time between each exercise to allow you to really absorb it. While it is tempting to do one exercise after another, it is better to take one exercise at a time.

Do not listen to the playback of these meditations while driving or operating heavy or dangerous machinery. Any type of meditation will slow the activity of the brain. While this is pleasurable and necessary for the imagery to do its work, it will also focus your mind solely on what you are visualizing. Obviously, if you are driving or operating other dangerous equipment, your attention must be on what you are doing, not on what you are imaging.

You may also find that you feel a little "spacey" for about 10 minutes after you have finished the meditations. This is normal. It takes about that amount of time for your brain activity to speed back up to its normal waking levels. To speed up your mental activity, make sure you put your attention on your physical body.

Feel sensations. Really look at what is around you. Listen to the quality of the sounds you hear. Revel in taste and scent. Mental focus on your body and physical activity will rev up your brain to its normal waking levels.

The exercises below will often prompt you to make specific intentions. You have the choice of repeating the intention in the first person, such as, "I intend (fill in the blank)..." Or, when an intention is prompted, you can simply say, "Yes, that" or "Yes, I intend that." For example, if the prompt is something like, "Make the intention that your inner wisdom teach you how to be balanced and healthy while being safe." if you are listening to a playback, you can say to yourself, "Yes, I intend that" instead of repeating the entire sentence or phrase.

Of course, you always have the option of saying no. If you are not ready to learn or if anything seems wrong for you, always follow your own intuition. Remember, your intuition is that gut feeling, inner knowing or voice inside of you that is calm, loving and balanced. If you have feelings or inner messages that are filled with fear, anger, etc., it is usually your ego or fear. This is okay. Don't try to fight the fear. Simply ask yourself what you need to know about the fear. Become curious. Intend health and balance for yourself. Intend goodness and be kind and gentle with yourself. There is no race or contest for you to win. You will grow and learn at your own pace.

These exercises are meant to invoke your ability to access and partner with your natural ability to use positive love based energy to keep you safe and grow into your best self. Use the book in the way that best allows you to clearly and vividly imagine all that is described below. Some of the imagery invokes spiritual ideas or metaphors. If you are a spiritual or religious person, use your creativity to tailor the meditations to integrate your belief system into the meditations. These meditations should support you in getting the best out of your spiritual and/or religious life. If you are not a spiritual or religious person, this may present you with a new opportunity to delve into what it means for you to live as a being in ways that bring you deeper meaning and fulfillment. It is my hope that each person who reads this book will be inspired to find new ways to thrive, enjoy and experience enhanced safety and security in their lives.

Let us begin.

Exercise 1: General Defense

The purpose of this exercise is to introduce you to the concept of energetic defense through positive energy. Many, if not most of us have unconscious strategies that send energy outward in ways we hope will keep us safe. This might come in the form of attack, submission, hiding or something else. People might give away power or attempt to suppress the power of others. People adopt these strategies in self defense.

If you are interested in what those strategies might look like from the point of view of energy, do an internet search for "Barbara Brennan energy defense," and you will find images that show unhealthy ways to use energy for safety. The following exercise is meant to stop the dysfunctional back and forth energy strategies and teach you how to sync up with the kinds of positive energies that repel unsafe, dysfunctional energies. This gives you the opportunity to transform your inner rules and perspectives about how to best experience safety and security in your life. Because this learning comes from your own inner wisdom, it is the wisdom and teaching that is exactly right for you.

Grounding Meditation

Do this meditation seated in a chair, with your feet flat on the floor. If you like, you can lay down during the meditation, but if you find yourself falling asleep, you may choose to sit while doing these meditations. Always intend that your meditations be gentle, balanced and healthy for you. Please note that the following meditations include requests or intentions for learning and healing. You do not have to repeat each request or intention in full. Instead, when you read or hear the suggested intention or request, simply say to yourself, "Yes, I intend that."

Take a deep breath and close your eyes. Feel your body relax. Now, imagine a beautiful field of light above your head. This light is white or golden, brilliant and pure. Allow and intend this beautiful light to flow down into your head, filling it; down into your neck and throat and into your shoulders, arms, and hands. This warm, bright light flows down into your chest, filling your lungs and heart space with light. It goes down through your solar plexus into your belly, into your whole back, into your hips and down into your legs. This light flows through your legs, knees, lower legs, ankles, and into your feet, filling all those spaces with light.

The light flows out of your feet in a white golden beam of light. It goes down through the floor, down through the whole house or building to the foundation, down through the foundation and into the earth. The light flows down, down, down through the rock and the dirt, through the sand and the water, down through all the layers of the earth, speeding its way to the place where you connect with earth energies. This is where you connect to all of your understandings of what it means to live on the earth, and in the universe and in your own being. You may see, feel or sense a pulsing light deep within the earth there. The golden white beam of light merges with the earth energies there.

And now, you see a stream of light emerge from this place, moving upward, speeding up, up, up, through the layers of the earth, moving higher and higher, up through the rock and the dirt, up through the sand and the water, up through the foundation of the house or building, up through the floor and into the soles of your feet. You feel, see or sense this beautiful earth energy fill your feet. It is clean and pure, calming, yet vital. It is the energy that makes the trees grow and all of life generate and regenerate in great abundance.

This beautiful earth energy flows up into your lower legs, your knees, your upper legs and into your hips. It fills your hips, your abdomen, your back and chest, your heart, your shoulders and your arms. The earth energy moves up and flows up into your neck and throat, into your head, filling those spaces, and it goes up, out of your head, showering around you, filling the field of energy that surrounds you, bringing the calm and peace and vitality of the earth energy to all the spaces that surround you.

You can feel the flow of golden white light descending from your head to your feet, and the flow of earth energy flowing from your feet to your head in a gentle, fulfilling flow of light. Take a moment to sit in the flow of this soothing energy.

Now, imagine yourself in a beautiful place in nature. It's a lovely day, with the sun shining and a light breeze. Allow yourself to feel the breeze as it gently moves against your skin, and to smell the air. You feel the soft earth under your feet, under your toes. You hear the sounds of nature all around you. Take a moment to see everything around you. See what is far away, and see what is close to you. Reach out and touch something that is close to you. Feel its texture. Smell the air and feel the sunlight. Take a moment to simply enjoy this place. Now, come back to your body, back to full awareness, take a deep breath and open your eyes.

Imagery Meditation--Part One

Again, you are seated or lying down, relaxed, with your eyes closed. Take a few deep breaths and reconnect with the positive flow of energy circulating through your body and the energy bubble that surrounds you. Reconnect with your place in nature. Again, feel the sunlight, and the breeze and feel the joy of this place. Now, you decide to wander and to walk along a path and explore. This path may be made of dirt or gravel or some other substance. Feel your feet walking on the path. You see plants or trees or flowers that line the path, You smell the scents, and you hear sounds all around you. And you notice that as the path curves, up ahead you see a big, beautiful house or castle with a tall, wide spire rising impossibly high up, up, up, into the sunlight. As you get closer, you notice more details about this house or castle.

You finally approach the front door and place the palm of your hand on the panel next to the entrance. When the door opens, you step into the house. You see the wide staircase in front of you, and you go up, up, up into the wide, airy, light filled stairwell. You continue to go up, and each step seems to give you energy so that you can speed up the stairs as fast as you like, almost floating upward. You notice that the walls of this wide staircase emit light that has an essence of happiness and ease. Your heart, your skin, your bones and organs begin to match and then sing with that same energy of joy and vitality.

You finally reach a landing and step into a room that contains many curious machines and controls and knobs of all kinds. You find a machine with a platform, and you step onto the platform and turn it on. As it gently shakes or vibrates, the machine easily loosens any heavy, dark or uncomfortable feeling in or around your body. You find that this vibration or shaking brings you even more ease, even more joy and even more comfort as tensions, or heaviness, lift and float away.

And now, you feel ready to move onward and upward. You turn off the machine and find another stairway that leads you up higher. This circular stair takes you to the top of the spire, to a room that is lit by an enormous crystal embedded into the ceiling above. Notice how beautiful the crystal is and how it seems to emanate an energy that is revitalizing and pure. You somehow know that in this room, with this crystal, you can connect to your own highest inner wisdom.

Allow yourself to sense the energy from this crystal. You might see a light coming from the crystal, flowing to you, around you and connecting to you. Or you might have a pleasant or relaxing sensation, or you might experience a knowing or hear wisdom from your inner voice giving you ideas, knowings or goodness. The more you connect to these energies, the more you merge with them. The more you merge with them, the more you feel in sync with them. The more you feel in sync with them, the more you learn and understand from your inner wisdom. You know that this understanding is so deep, it does not have to register with your conscious mind, it registers with the unconscious parts of you that are responsible for your energetic defenses. As these unconscious parts of your being sync up with your inner wisdom, you may see, feel or experience that you are actually drawn up into the crystal, experiencing and becoming one with these beautiful, wise energies.

Now make the intention that the energies in this crystal teach you and your natural energy defenses what you need to know about your right to, ability to and how to defend yourself energetically. Now, see, feel or experience the energy come down from the crystal and surround you. It goes into every cell of your body, every molecule, and every gene. It goes into every corner of your mind, your heart and your gut, and it goes deeply into your heart, where your soul resides. It flows backwards behind you, as if it is filling the timeline of your life, all of your lives and all of the connections throughout time that form your thoughts, awareness and consciousness. And this light flows forward in front of you into all of your hopes, dreams, intentions and beliefs and all of the connections that will form your thoughts, awareness and consciousness. The light goes in all directions to your present. Now intend the bright beautiful energy from the crystal to permeate all the parts of who you are, in all the different aspects of your life, in all time, and even between your awareness of time, as in your sleep.

Reconnect with your experience of being at the top of the spire, experiencing the flow of energy through the crystal. The crystal energy, containing all this knowledge, now flows down through your body, down through your feet, down through the spire of the building, down into the earth, a hundred feet down into the bedrock and even further down into the earth where you connect to all of your understandings of what it means to live on the earth, and in the universe and in your own being. You may see, feel or sense a pulsing light deep within the earth there. Let all of the wisdom energy flow into this space and connect to the earth energies there. When you are ready, allow these energies, from this place, deep in the earth to flow up through the earth to you, to fill your body and your awareness. Now, allow this energy to radiate out to the space you hold around yourself. You are filled with, and surrounded by these integrated energies of wisdom and new learning.

For just a moment, come back to the awareness of your body. Come back to your room and back to your chair and back to your physical body. Take a deep breath and open your eyes. Let your mind rest for a moment and feel your body. When you are ready, let's go back to the meditation to learn and experience more.

Imagery Meditation--Part Two

Now, remember the house or castle with its spire and the room at the top of the spire. Remember the flow of your inner wisdom through the crystal. Remember receiving that flow of wisdom and allowing those energies to flow to the earth, to integrate there and to return to you and the bubble that surrounds you. Turn your attention back to the crystal at the top of the room. Make the intention that the crystal energy release and dissolve any past or future pain, fear, trauma or other discomfort regarding your safety and security. And ask the crystal to teach you how to allow your natural energy defenses to dissolve, resolve and release any thoughts or emotions that block your safety and security.

Now see, feel or experience the wisdom energy flow down from the crystal to fill your body, and all the area around you. It flows to the places where you experience physical pain, emotional pain or spiritual pain. As these pains or memories of pain release and lift away, they flow up to the crystal or down to the earth to be transformed into something better. You watch, feel or experience the crystal's light flow into all your senses, clearing them of pain. This might be through your eyes, ears, nose, mouth, hands, feet, heart, gut or any other part of you that relates to your physical being or your intuition.

You see, feel or experience the healing energy flow deep, deep, deep into your heart, releasing emotional pain, and deeper still into your soul, releasing energies there. The light flows out the back of your heart throughout all the connections you have with the past, going through you and those who have gone before you. The pains or wounds there lift and float away. When that is complete, you see, feel or experience the light flow out the front of your heart to your connections to the future you. All the pains and all the fears of pain release and float away. Now allow the bright beautiful energy from the crystal to permeate all the parts of your present experience, flowing in every direction around you.

The crystal energy now flows down through your feet, down through the spire of the building, down into the earth where you connect to earth energies. Let that wisdom energy from the crystal flow to this space and let the earth energies there mix and mingle with all of the wisdom and healing. Now, allow these energies to flow back to you, bringing them up into your body and the space around you.

Now turn your attention to the crystal at the top of the room. Make the intention that your inner wisdom, through the crystal, teaches and guides you and your natural energy defenses how to work together, how to use and accept positive energies to create safety and security and how to do so with integrity, honor and effectiveness. See, feel or experience the energy flow down from the crystal and surround you. The energy goes into every cell of your body and every corner of your mind, your heart and your gut. It flows into your emotions, into your soul, and backward and forward through time. You may see, feel or sense this energy of learning fill you up and fill up your present experience. You experience this energy permeating your whole being, teaching you how to live your best and happiest life without pain and fear and with the natural energy defenses that are now a natural part of you.

The crystal energy now flows down through your feet, down through the spire of the building, down into the earth, down to the place where you connect to the earth. As you experience the wisdom energy flowing down to this space, you may experience more understanding, guidance and support. Now, feel, see or sense the earth energy flowing back up to you and the space around you and tune into the energies of love and support flowing from your inner wisdom, through the crystal and from the earth to your whole being. As you drink in this energy, allow it to flow into every aspect of your being.

Take a moment to feel gratitude for these energies, for the learning and for the healing. We now remember all that we have done, the place in nature, the house or castle, with its stairway, vibrating and easing machinery and the beautiful crystal at the top of the spire. You remember syncing up with your inner wisdom and its teachings about your permission and ability to have and use energy defenses. You remember how you released pain, trauma and fear from your physical and emotional self, from your soul, your past, your future and all the dimensions of your being. You remember grounding the learning and healing into the earth itself and receiving supportive earth energies. You also remember learning how to accept, claim and use your energy defenses through positive energies with the support of your inner wisdom and the earth.

Now it's time to come back to the room and back to your chair. You can leave the crystal room, going down through the other rooms, down the staircase, out of the building, along the path, back to your place in nature. And now come back to your room, back to your chair, back to your body and back to your current time and place. Feel your feet flat on the floor. Move your shoulders around and take a deep breath in and out. Slowly, in your own time, open your eyes.

Follow up questions

How easy or difficult was it for you to follow the meditation? If it was difficult, what changes might you make to have an easier experience? (For example, you might: find a more peaceful or comfortable setting, practice meditating, take breaks during the meditation, change the playback, practice good hydration, do the meditation at a different time of day or get help from an energy healer or guided imagery professional).

Describe the place in nature, castle and crystal room.

What were your thoughts and sensations while you were experiencing the learning and healing through energy?

What insights, if any, did you gain?

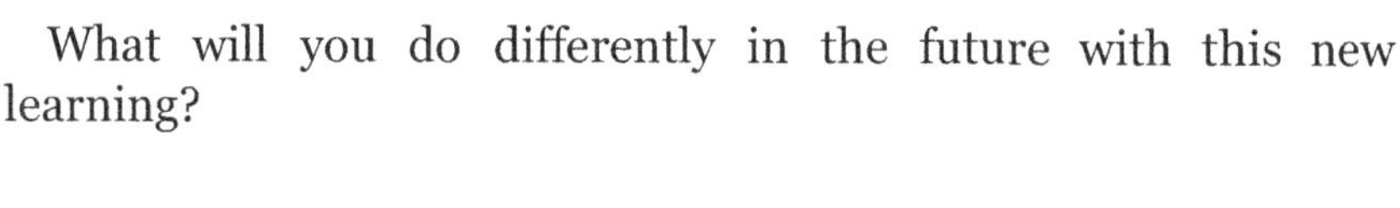

What will you do differently in the future with this new learning?

Do you feel safer? If so, how?

Note: *If the above exercise was difficult for you, you might want to skip to the Resistance exercises and then repeat the exercise above.*

Exercise 2: Know Yourself with Limits and Boundaries

The term boundaries has taken hold in recent years. Often, when people talk about boundaries, they describe the ability to say no or the ability to stand up for yourself. While this is great, it often places the focus on the outer world. The following exercise will teach you how to change your attention to yourself. As you do so, your natural energy boundaries have more space and more energy to heal and develop. You don't have to build boundaries out of your will or anger. It is better to come to a place of health and balance in your boundaries. When you take the responsibility for cleaning up your inner energy space and allow yourself to learn and grow, your boundaries will be more natural, self loving, healthy and balanced.

Grounding Meditation

Do this meditation seated in a chair, with your feet flat on the floor. If you like, you can lay down during the meditation, but if you find yourself falling asleep, you may choose to sit while doing these meditations. Always intend that your meditations be gentle, balanced and healthy for you. Please note that the following meditations include requests or intentions for learning and healing. You do not have to repeat each request or intention in full. Instead, when you read or hear the suggested intention or request, simply say to yourself, "Yes, I intend that."

Close your eyes and take a deep breath. Remember the beautiful field of light above your head. You see the white or golden color and how brilliant and pure it is. Allow this light to descend down to your head, and notice what you feel in connecting with this light. The light touches the crown of your head, and fills your head. It goes down into your neck and throat and down into your shoulders, arms, and hands, filling those spaces. This warm, comforting light flows down into your chest, filling your lungs, chest and heart space with light. It goes down through your solar plexus into your gut, into your whole back, into your hips and down into your legs. This light flows through and fills your legs, knees, lower legs, ankles, and feet.

The light flows out of your feet, down through the floor, down through the whole house or building to the foundation, down through the foundation and into the earth. The light flows down, down, down through the rock and the dirt, through the sand and the water, down through the layers of the earth, speeding its way to that special place where you naturally connect to the earth. In this place, you find meaning, you connect more clearly with your inner self and gain new insights about what it means to live on the earth and to live as a being in creation. Allow the beautiful golden white light to flow to this space and connect with the energies there. Allow the earth energies to connect with the golden white light. See, feel or experience the swirling and merging of all of these energies.

And now, you allow this integrated, merged energy to flow upward, speeding up, up, up, through the earth, moving higher and higher, up through the rock and the dirt, up through the sand and the water, up through the foundation of the house or building, up through the floor and into the soles of your feet. You feel, see or sense this beautiful earth energy fill your feet. It is clean and pure, calming yet vital. You understand that this is the energy that makes the trees grow and all of life generate and regenerate in great abundance.

This beautiful earth energy flows up into your lower legs, your knees, your upper legs and into your hips. It fills your hips, your abdomen, your back, your chest, your heart, your shoulders and arms. The earth energy moves and flows up into your neck and throat, into your head, filling those spaces and up out of your head, showering around you, filling the field of energy that surrounds you, bringing the calm and peace and vitality of the earth energy to all the spaces that surround you. You notice that there is a bubble of light that surrounds you, and that the earth energy, showering around you, fills this bubble. You can feel the flow of golden white light descending from your head to your feet, and the flow of earth energy flowing from your feet to your head and your bubble in a gentle, fulfilling flow of light. Take a moment to sit in the flow of these soothing energies. Now, come back to full awareness, take a deep breath, and open your eyes.

Imagery Meditation

Again, you are seated or lying down, relaxed, with your eyes closed. Take a few deep breaths and reconnect with the positive flow of energy circulating through your body and the energy bubble that surrounds you. Now imagine that you could shrink yourself down, very small, so small that you can easily fit inside your heart. Imagine that you are that small version of you inside your heart. Imagine or pretend as if your heart can feel love flowing from the earth up into your heart. As that small you, go to that place in your heart and see, feel or experience that love. You might take a piece of that love and eat it as if it were food, or drink it as if the love energy was a drinking fountain. You might jump into that energy as if it was a swimming pool or soaking tub. Or you might see that energy transform and grow or blossom, with you merging with it and becoming one with this transformation. See, feel and experience how this energy of love is just for you, no one else. It was crafted for you and can be experienced by you alone. It brings with it learning and knowledge about who you are as an individual person. It teaches you about the difference between love and other energies. As you merge with this energy of love, you begin to match that same energy frequency. You allow yourself to match that same energy frequency of love. As you do so, you might see, feel or experience other energies release or fall away. This is okay. These energies that are releasing fall away because they do not match love. They do not match the goodness of love for you. You are vibrating to the rhythm of love.

If this is hard for you, ask your inner wisdom to readjust your perspectives and beliefs so that you trust yourself and trust that you are worthy and deserving of this love and of being protected and cherished. Allow this wisdom to sink into every cell of your body, every molecule, and every gene. It goes into every corner of your mind, your heart and your gut and deeply into your heart, where your soul resides. It flows backwards behind you, as if it is filling the timeline of your life, all of your lives and all of the connections throughout time that form your thoughts, awareness and consciousness. And this light flows forward in front of you into all of your hopes, dreams, intentions and beliefs and all of the connections that will form your thoughts, awareness and consciousness. It flows to the present and to areas of your consciousness that do not experience time. Allow the wisdom to flow down to the earth where you allow the earth energies to integrate with the wisdom. Let the integrated energies return to you and the bubble that surrounds you.

Return to the love energy in your heart. Allow yourself to sync up with the love and the love to sink into every part of you, all of time, your soul, your genetic material and your whole being. Now, feel all the energies of you, the parts of you, the past, present and future yous, your heart and soul, your mind and gut, your whole body with its genetic material, senses and physical abilities. Now claim it all, including the love that is just for you by saying with your heart, "This is me." Imagine that your statement goes out the front of your heart to your bubble and its connection to your future. It goes out the back of your heart to the part of the bubble that relates to your past. The statement, "This is me" goes up out of your head to the part of your bubble that connects you to your spiritual source, and it goes from your heart down through your feet to the part of your bubble that connects to the earth. It goes in all directions to fill present time.

Now, ask your inner wisdom and the love energy to teach you what you need to know about the difference between the energies of your being and other energies and how to experience limits and boundaries with integrity, wisdom, good health and safety.

Feel yourself absorb and become one with the energy of this teaching. Now ask your inner wisdom and the love energy to teach your natural energy defenses how to create energetic limits and boundaries fueled by love and guided by wisdom and also to teach you how to accept that support. As you allow this energy of learning to flow into your system, you see, feel or experience the love energy surround and fill you. You see, feel or experience the wisdom energy flow to your whole being, throughout time and through your body, genetics and soul. This energy naturally grounds down to the earth, to that place where you connect with the earth and you allow the earth energies to integrate and merge with the teaching. And this renewed energy returns to you, filling you, the bubble that surrounds you and your natural energy defenses.

Now notice that the love energy flows out into the bubble of light that surrounds you. Intend the love energy to teach you and your natural energy defenses how to make that bubble your own, creating limits and boundaries throughout this bubble, knowing that it is all done with integrity and honor. Now allow your natural energy defenses to create the limits and boundaries within your bubble. You may see, feel or experience some energies filling in or draining away, and as you do so, also stay in the flow of the love energy, allowing it to fill the bubble with love that was created for you alone. It fills in places that were hurt or lacking. It fills in places of self-generated unkindness. It fills in places that may have been out of balance, out of truth and out of alignment with love for you. These places begin to melt or change or transform as they match a better frequency.

Again, allow the love energy to fill your heart, and with your heart say, "With this love, I claim my bubble." Allow the energy of this statement to go out your heart in front and in back, in all directions, out your feet and head and fill up the bubble with this truth and this reality. Allow the love and your natural energy defenses to make it so.

Take a moment to feel gratitude for these energies, for the love, the learning and for the healing. We now remember all that we have done, shrinking down and experiencing the unique love for you coming from the earth to your heart. You remember learning how to trust yourself and your worthiness. You remember syncing up with the love and how it taught your natural energy defenses how to make limits and boundaries. You remember how the love brought healing and how you claimed that love by stating it through your heart. You also remember the love filling the bubble around you and how you claimed your bubble with love and the wise and honorable support of your natural energy defenses.

Now it's time to come back to the room and back to your chair, back to your body and back to your current time and place. Feel your feet flat on the floor. Move your shoulders around and take a deep breath in and out. Slowly, in your own time, open your eyes.

Follow up questions

How did you experience the love energy?

Did you feel or experience the uniqueness of the love for you? If so, what does that mean to you?

What part or parts were easy and what parts were hard?

Did it feel like you claimed the bubble of energy that surrounds you?

What insights, if any, did you gain?

Did this help you feel safer? Please describe.

Exercise 3: Outside Your Sphere of Influence

Grounding Meditation

Do this meditation seated in a chair, with your feet flat on the floor. If you like, you can lay down during the meditation, but if you find yourself falling asleep, you may choose to sit while doing these meditations. Always intend that your meditations be gentle, balanced and healthy for you. Please note that the following meditations include requests or intentions for learning and healing. You do not have to repeat each request or intention in full. Instead, when you read or hear the suggested intention or request, simply say to yourself, "Yes, I intend that."

Take a few deep breaths and close your eyes. Feel the heaviness of your body supported by your chair. Feel your feet flat against the floor. Feel the weight of your arms by your sides. Feel the weight of your shoulders relaxing down. Your head, supported by your spine, is balanced, kept upright by the natural action of your muscles, tendons and ligaments, working with your spine to create a perfect foundation for your head. Your tongue has dropped to the bottom of your mouth. Your eyelids are heavy. The weight of your physical being is held by the tug of gravity toward the earth. Feel the pull of gravity. Allow yourself to feel that magnetic pull.

Your body, made up of molecules, atoms and particles is feeling, responding to and immersed in the earth's gravitational field. This gravitational field extends upward and outward, tugging and pulling on everything on the earth's surface, all the air, water, dust and gases. It pulls on all the layers of the atmosphere. It pulls on the moon, the other planets and the sun. And in perfect balance, the sun and planets and moon have their own gravitational pull. These forces, in perfect harmony, allow the planets and moons, sun and stars to nestle into orbits, tugging and balancing while you, nestled into your chair, are held fast to the earth by its gravity, its gentle, gentle, falling pull. Name a sensation or emotion you would like to release. Intend that gravity pulls it down, out and away. You allow it to fall away and you see, feel or sense the release as it is pulled down. Now, allow your natural energy defenses to bring goodness to the area emptied out. Intend that love fills in that area. You may see the love come from your own heart, the earth or your spiritual source. See, feel or experience love fill in that space. Take a moment to sit in the flow of this loving, soothing energy. Now, come back to full awareness, take a deep breath, and open your eyes.

Imagery Meditation

Take a deep breath and close your eyes. Return to the image of you, feeling the pull of the earth, knowing the sun and moon and planets also exert gravity of their own. You feel the tug of gravity and also the feel of balance as you let your chair support you. Now, pretend as if the force pulling you toward the earth was actually the force, pull and attraction of unconditional love. Imagine or pretend as if all of the choreography of orbits within the solar system was a dance of love, pulling the sun and planets and moons into harmonious circles. And also imagine that you are a part of this choreography of love. The closer you are, the more you feel the unconditional love. And the sun, being so big and so impactful brings so much love. The sun and earth have an abundance of love that is tugging on you, attracting you. If you like, you can choose to send an abundance of love to the sun which might be a metaphor for your spiritual source, and to the earth, which gives you life. Take a moment to realize the abundance of love you hold for people, places and things in your life. If you like, you can send an abundance of love to who or what you love, seeing these people, places or things in an orbit around you. You might actually see that you are surrounded by a bubble of light and that outside your bubble, there are people, places and things orbiting you like satellites. Notice that there is an outer edge to these orbits. Everything within that boundary is your sphere of influence. Your energies directly touch the people, places and things within your sphere of influence.

Now ask your inner wisdom to teach you how to stop feeding energy into the orbits of people, places and things that do not belong within your sphere of influence and to teach you how to allow them to naturally and easily leave your sphere of influence. You might see, feel or experience a golden white light begin to flow into your head, into your body, filling your body. It goes into every cell, every molecule, and every gene. It goes into every corner of your mind, your heart and your gut and deeply into your heart, where your soul resides. It flows backwards behind you, as if it is filling the timeline of your life, all of your lives and all of the connections throughout time that form your thoughts, awareness and consciousness. And this light flows forward in front of you into all of your hopes, dreams, intentions and beliefs and all of the connections that will form your thoughts, awareness and consciousness. It goes to present time and to any aspect of you that is outside the awareness of time.

Now imagine that the light and energy now flows down through your body, down through your feet, down into the earth, a hundred feet down into the bedrock and even further down into the earth where you connect to all of your understandings of what it means to live on the earth, and in the universe and in your own being. Allow the earth energies there to mix, mingle and integrate with the wisdom energy. And now you see, feel or experience the integrated energy to flow up from the earth to you and fill your body and the bubble of light that surrounds you. Now ask your natural energy defenses to implement this new knowledge. See, feel or experience the falling away or lessening of certain energies, emotions or thoughts. Focus on feelings of allowing your natural energy defenses to do it all. You might see, feel or experience soothing energies flowing to you from your natural energy defenses. Now intend and allow love from the earth and if you like, love from your spiritual source to fill in where those orbits used to be, healing and balancing, bringing life and wisdom. And if you like, you can give permission for new people, places and things that are exactly right for you to be drawn into your sphere of influence. Take a moment to experience these energies.

Now take stock. Notice that all of the people, places and things in orbit around you belong in your sphere of influence and you belong in their sphere of influence. There might be shared love or goodness or learning or creating or inspiration or some other reason they are in your sphere of influence. Notice how you feel about the rightness of these people, places or things within your sphere of influence and the rightness of you within their spheres of influence. And just like our solar system has a border, notice that there is a border around your sphere of influence. Ask your inner wisdom or higher power to teach you what you need to know about the boundary around your sphere of influence, how to maintain that boundary and keep it healthy and how to do so with honor and integrity. As before, you allow that wisdom to fill you up in every particle of your body, deep into your heart, mind and gut, out the back and front of your heart, to your present, to your experience of no time and to your soul. Now allow the wisdom and learning to flow down to the earth, to mix and mingle there and the earth energy returns back to you. Ask your natural energy defenses to heal and maintain the healthy boundaries around your sphere of influence. Take the time to see, feel or experience this process of allowing.

Now turn your attention to your experience of belonging, how the people, places and things inside your sphere of influence belong there and how you belong in their spheres. Notice how you belong on the earth, how you belong in the solar system, how you belong in the galaxy, how you belong in the universe and, if you like, how you belong in the light of your own higher power. You might feel a sensation of belonging or the flow of belonging energy flowing to you. If you like, you can ask your natural energy defenses to dissolve, resolve and release any energies that block your experience of belonging.

Take a moment to feel gratitude for these energies, for the love, the learning and for the healing. We now remember all that we have done, how you visualized the orbits and pulls of love in the solar system and in your life. You remember receiving and sending love and you remember learning how to stop sending energy to the orbits of the things, events and people who do not belong in your sphere of influence. You remember how your natural energy defenses easily removed what does not belong and what it felt like to have the orbits of what does belong in your life and perhaps new people, places or things that belong in your sphere of influence. You remember what it felt like to allow your natural energy defenses to heal and maintain the boundaries around your sphere of influence, and what it felt like to embrace the feelings of belonging.

Now it's time to come back to the room and back to your chair, back to your body and back to your current time and place. Feel your feet flat on the floor. Move your shoulders around and take a deep breath in and out. Slowly, in your own time, open your eyes.

Follow up questions

What did you see, feel or experience when visualizing the orbits of people, places and things around you?

Do you feel that you completely released all of the people, places or things that do not belong in your sphere of influence? If not, who or what do you still need to release?

When imagining your "sphere of influence", what was your experience?

What might you do differently after having experienced this imagery meditation?

What insights, if any, did you gain?

Did this help you feel safer? Please describe.

Bonus Section

If you still feel attached to people, places and things that you believe do not belong in your sphere of influence, perhaps there is more for you to learn and more your natural energy defenses can do for you in finding balance and ease with those experiences that do belong in your life. In the following exercise, you will learn how to allow your natural energy defenses to "massage" unhealthy attachments in ways that dissolve them. In massage therapy, the gua sha technique, a light, fast scrubbing of the skin is used to shear off adhesions that stick the skin and muscle together. When those adhesions dissolve, the muscles can stretch and contract naturally and blood can flow into the area, bringing healing. In the same way, you will learn how to allow your natural energy defenses to bring a faster vibration of energy into areas of unhealthy attachment. This faster moving energy vibrates in such a way to dissolve or shear off attachments that no longer serve your highest good. The energy of your inner wisdom will fill that space, helping you understand what you need to know about the attachments, the healing and how to live in a better inner environment of energy.

Bonus Meditation

Find a quiet place to sit. Make yourself comfortable there. Close your eyes and take a nice, deep breath. Return to your place in nature. Reconnect to the flow of wisdom from your inner wisdom. Recall how it felt at the top of the spire, receiving energy from the crystal. Remember the energy flowing down to you. Now, in your place of nature, feel that flow of wisdom filling your head, flowing down through your neck and throat, down into your whole body, down through your legs and feet and into the earth. Allow it to flow down to the place where you connect with earth energies and let the earth energies flow back up to you, through your body, out the top of your head and shower around you, filling the bubble that surrounds you. Now, reconnect with the image, feeling and knowing of your sphere of influence, knowing that you belong within this sphere of influence.

Now, make the intention to see or know anything within this sphere that does not belong. Make the intention to see or know the attachments that do not belong. Now, make the intention that your natural energy defenses go to those attachments and apply the exact right vibrations of energies that will dissolve and resolve those attachments, along with any emotions or sensations that are connected to the attachments. See, feel or experience your natural energy defenses bring these new vibrations to these attachments. At the same time, ask your inner wisdom to teach you what you need to know about the attachments and about their release. You are letting your natural energy defenses bring in new, higher vibrations of energy and you are allowing the wisdom and learning to flow into your head, your body, your heart, soul, gut, time, no time and the entire blueprint of your physical, emotional and spiritual being. You may see, feel or experience your body or your energy field being vibrated or massaged. Or, you may experience the changes in the sphere of influence around you. It may feel as if the learning you are receiving is at a very deep and unconscious level. Allow yourself to be at peace in not having to know consciously what is being changed or healed.

You may see or experience the difference between your energy field and the fields of energy of the people, places or things that do not belong in your sphere of influence. Allow yourself to not match those other energy fields, to not be in sync, to not connect. If you like, you can ask your inner wisdom to give you the perspectives and beliefs that will allow you to be at ease in not matching, syncing or connecting to the energy fields that do not belong in your sphere of influence.

Now you allow all of this wisdom, all of these changes, all of the healing and all of the ease flow down through your body, down through your feet and into the earth. It flows down, down, down to the place where you connect with earth energies. You allow the earth energies to integrate and synthesize these wisdom and energies. Now allow the integrated energies to flow back to you. They flow up through the earth, up into your feet, legs, body, head and out into the bubble that surrounds you. Now take stock of your sphere of influence. You may feel a shift in the experience of rightness or belonging within this sphere. It may seem as if the energies from your bubble radiate out to the whole sphere of influence, bringing more balance and ease.

Now it's time to come back to your room and back to your chair, but before you do, let's remember all you have done. You remember your place in nature and how you could connect with the flow of wisdom and your connection to the earth there. You remember your natural energy defenses massaging your attachments with high vibrational energies and how your inner wisdom supported healing and transformation through teaching you what you need to know in order to release the attachments, not match or sync with them and live at ease without them. You remember what it felt like to ground these changes into the earth and claim them for your own by allowing the earth to synchronize and integrate those energies. You remember allowing the synchronized energies to flow out from your bubble to your sphere of influence, bringing more balance and ease in living with the people, places and things that belong in your sphere of influence.

Now come back to the room and back to your chair. Feel your body. Feel the support of your chair. Allow your body to move. Shrug your shoulders, move your fingers and toes, and when you are ready, open your eyes.

Second Bonus Section

Another way to view your sphere of influence is to see it as your sphere of attention. In this meditation, you will learn how to shift your attention to what is good to you. You will also learn how to release negative attention from others. Imagine the changes you could make if you could feel safe enough to drop your attention away from the haters or judgers or chaos makers. Imagine how much more energy and joy you could experience.

For many of us, this is difficult because we carry beliefs such as, "Keep your friends close, but your enemies closer." In other words, you might feel the need to be constantly vigilant regarding the people, places or things that you feel are threats. Those threats might be in current time or in the past or in an imaginary future. This drains the energy you have available to create or even think about the experiences you love most. In this meditation, you will learn how to replace your emotion-filled attention with objectivity. Instead of pretending that threats are invisible, you will simply shift your perspective to the kind of objectivity that allows you to connect to your inner wisdom to help you understand what is important for you to learn and how to live in a sphere of attention that stops feeding attention to the things that feel like a threat.

Second Bonus Meditation

Find a place to sit and relax. Close your eyes. Let your shoulders drop. Uncurl your toes. Relax your fingers. Take a deep breath. Feel the tug of gravity and remember your image of the solar system, galaxy and universe filled with planets, moons and suns moving in rhythms of gravity and motion. Remember what it felt like to imagine that all of the force of gravity was actually the attraction and pull of unconditional love. Imagine that the tug of gravity that you feel now is simply the force and attraction of the earth's unconditional love for you. Imagine and feel that you are in a force field of love. Now extend your attention out to your bubble and then farther out to your own sphere of influence. This sphere contains all of the people, places and things that influence you and that you and your life impact in return.

Ask your inner wisdom to show you how this sphere of influence is also your sphere of attention. Allow this flow of wisdom and learning to flow into your head and down into your body. It goes to your whole mind, heart and gut. You see, feel or experience it go deeply into your heart and fill your soul. You see it fill your past, present, future and even your experience of no time. You allow it into your cells, molecules, genetic material and every particle of your being and you ground this energy down into the earth where you allow the earth energy to integrate and synthesize it. As you allow the integrated energy to return to you, your body and the bubble that surrounds you, allow yourself to see or know how your sphere of influence is your sphere of attention. See how the quality of the attention to and from you shapes this sphere of attention. Notice how the quality of the attention to and from you impacts your happiness, ease and capacity for joy and safety.

Ask your inner wisdom to shift your perspectives. Ask that your attention to the negativities in your sphere of attention shift to a perspective of objectivity. And ask your inner wisdom to teach you what you need to know about your own beliefs and motivations and how to release your emotions and replace them with objectivity. Again, you allow this wisdom and healing to flow into all of you, your whole mind, body, soul, all of time and your experience outside the flow of time.

Now notice the area or areas where you feel a sense of threat or negative attention. Notice that in those areas, you have sensors or receptors that sync up with the threat or negative attention. Ask your natural energy defenses to cover those sensors or receptors with love. You might see or experience the love energy as a sort of blanket or salve or force field. Notice that the love within the blanket, salve or force field contains a sort of attention. Allow yourself to experience the loving attention flowing to you. This attention should feel easy, warm, kind or gentle.

If this is difficult for you, ask your inner wisdom to teach you how to be safe and feel safe experiencing this loving attention. If you like, you can ask your inner wisdom to readjust your beliefs to allow you to experience loving attention, to trust yourself, trust your worthiness and to trust the loving attention and energy. Again, you allow this wisdom into your whole being. As you experience the loving attention more clearly or deeply, you might notice that your receptors or sensors are changing. Notice how the frequency or quality of your own energy within those areas transforms. You might experience the loving attention as waves. Allow your own energy within your receptors to match those waves of love. To do this, you relax and allow your energy to match the energy of the loving attention.

You might notice that a new energy of trust or self-trust is flowing into your being, replacing your fears or other emotions. Or, you may see, feel or experience energies of worthiness flowing to you, filling your heart, your body and the bubble that surrounds you. Allow yourself to match all of these positive energies. As you match the energies of self-trust and worthiness, you might notice yourself opening more and more to the loving attention brought by your natural energy defenses. Perhaps it flows into your soul or into your genetics. Maybe you see or experience it flowing to your perception of time and no time. You might see it fill your heart, mind or gut and then radiate out in all directions.

Return your attention to the receptors or sensors that previously received negativity. Notice if they have changed. Perhaps they have transformed to love receptors or perhaps they have disappeared or changed in some other way. Now return to your experience of objectivity about the negative people, places or things within your sphere of attention. Allow the objectivity to flow to you and fill you up. Notice how it gives you a different perspective. You may feel more distance or detachment. You might notice that now you are protected by your natural energy defenses, you have the security to ask your inner wisdom what is good for you to know about the negative people, places or things.

Now ask your inner wisdom to teach you how to live with this objectivity in healthy and balanced ways that allow you to have objectivity and compassion and integrity while being open to and safe with loving relationships in your life. Let that wisdom into your whole being, including your soul, genetics, time and even outside the flow of time. Now ground all of the learning, all of the changes, all of the objectivity, love, trust, worthiness and goodness down into the earth where the earth energies integrate and synthesize it all. Allow all of the integrated energies to flow back up to you, fill you and fill the bubble that surrounds you.

Take a moment to enjoy and feel gratitude for all of these loving, trusting energies and notice how you may feel more worthy and deserving of loving, positive attention and notice just how good that feels. Now it's time to come back to your room and back to your chair, but before you do, let's remember all we have done. You remember the force field of love that surrounded you and how your inner wisdom showed you your sphere of attention. You remember learning about objectivity and allowing that objectivity to free you from the negative things within your sphere of influence. You remember your natural energy defenses covering any receptors you had to the negative things within your attention and how those defenses brought loving attention to you. You remember learning how to trust yourself, your worthiness and the love that flowed to you. You remember what it felt like to feel self-trust and worthiness and loving attention. You remember what it felt like to feel objectivity for the negative things within your attention and how easy it was to ask for wisdom about these things. And you remember what it felt like to enjoy the flow of deservingness, trust and love. Now come back to your room and back to your chair. Feel your body. Move your fingers. Move your toes. Shrug your shoulder. Take a deep breath, and in your own time, open your eyes.

Inside Your Sphere of Influence

If outside your sphere of influence is that which does not belong, then the people, places or things inside your sphere of influence are there for a reason. Not all of them will be close to you or influence you in large ways. The people closest to you impact you the most and those farthest out, influence you the least. It is helpful to understand the different kinds of energy exchanges you have with the people, places and things near and far. We will explore this topic by visualizing different layers of your sphere of influence, seeing each layer with a different color.

Exercise 4: Community, Large and Small

Grounding Meditation

Do this meditation seated in a chair, with your feet flat on the floor. If you like, you can lay down during the meditation, but if you find yourself falling asleep, you may choose to sit while doing these meditations. Always intend that your meditations be gentle, balanced and healthy for you. Please note that the following meditations include requests or intentions for learning and healing. You do not have to repeat each request or intention in full. Instead, when you read or hear the suggested intention or request, simply say to yourself, "Yes, I intend that."

Take a deep breath and close your eyes. Take a few deep breaths and reconnect with the positive flow of energy circulating through your body and the energy bubble that surrounds you. Now, imagine yourself in your place of nature. It's a beautiful day, with the sun shining, with a light breeze. Allow yourself to feel the breeze as it gently moves against your skin, and to smell the air. You feel the soft earth under your feet, under your toes. You hear the sounds of nature all around you. In this beautiful place, you can easily connect to your inner wisdom and to the earth. Notice how, as you remember your own inner wisdom, you see, feel or experience an energy flowing to you and through you that is revitalizing and pure. You feel the warmth and goodness of this wisdom energy flowing down through your body. And as you relax more and more, that wisdom easily flows down to the place where you connect with earth energy. Now allow the earth energy to return to you and fill your body and your bubble. Take a moment to enjoy this circulation of energy, and when you are ready, take a deep breath and open your eyes.

Imagery Meditation

Again, you are seated or lying down, relaxed, with your eyes closed. Allow yourself to sense the flow of wisdom energy and earth energy. You might see a light flowing to you, around you and connecting to you. Or you might have pleasant, relaxing sensations, or you might experience a knowing or hear wisdom from your inner voice giving you ideas, knowings or goodness. The more you connect to these energies, the more you merge with them. The more you merge with them, the more you feel in sync with them. The more you feel in sync with them, the more you learn and understand from your inner wisdom. You know that this understanding is so deep, it does not have to register with your conscious mind, it registers with the unconscious parts of you that are responsible for your energetic defenses.

Now turn your attention to your sphere of influence. You see yourself in your place of nature with the bubble of light and energy around you. Outside of this bubble is your sphere of influence, like a much, much larger bubble, containing the energies that represent the people, places and things that belong to your sphere of influence. You begin to see that the sphere of influence contains different colored layers. The outer layer is a deep burgundy color, the next closer layer is magenta, a vibrant red pink color, the next closer layer is red, and the layer closest to your bubble is orange. The color of your own bubble might be white or golden, and you know that you can change the colors of these layers and the color of your own bubble whenever you like, but for now, we will let the colors be burgundy, magenta, red, orange and golden white.

Now ask your inner wisdom to teach you and your natural energy defenses what you need to know about the people, places and things in the burgundy layer of your sphere of influence. You see, feel or experience the energy of this wisdom flowing to you and surrounding you. It goes into every cell of your body, every molecule, and every gene. It goes into every corner of your mind, your heart and your gut and deeply into your heart, where your soul resides. It flows backwards behind you, as if it is filling the timeline of your life, all of your lives and all of the connections throughout time that form your thoughts, awareness and consciousness. And this light flows forward in front of you into all of your hopes, dreams, intentions and beliefs and all of the connections that will form your thoughts, awareness and consciousness. Intend the wisdom to flow to the present and to parts of your consciousness that do not experience time.

The energy, containing all this knowledge and wisdom, now flows down through your body, down through your feet, into the earth, a hundred feet down into the bedrock and even further down into the earth where you connect to all of your understandings of what it means to live on the earth, and in the universe and in your own being. The earth energies integrate and synthesize the wisdom and then you allow this integrated energy to flow up from the earth to you and fill your body and the bubble that surrounds you.

You might see, feel or experience the integrated energy flow out to the burgundy layer and shift the energies there. You notice that this layer contains your connections to the global community, your nation, your local community or other groups to which you belong. If you believe in past lifetimes or the connection to ancestors, you might see the integrated earth energies flow there or to places, real or imagined, that you have seen, but never visited or other things, real or imagined. As you allow these energies to flow, you might feel shifts or changes in yourself. You might notice that as you change, your connections in the burgundy layer change. Notice as you allow these energies to flow, your will is passive. These energies flow in support of your health, balance and ease without you having to work, or send energy or give up any of your personal energy or power. Notice how the healing and changes are within you, and that the changes in your sphere of influence are simply a readjustment in response to your inner transformation. Notice also that as energies exchange between you and this burgundy layer, your natural energy defenses surround your bubble and protect you.

Ask your natural energy defenses to dissolve, resolve and release any distressing or unhealthy judgements, emotions, rules or obligations that you hold in relation to the burgundy layer of your sphere of influence. You might see, feel or experience your natural energy defenses focus on and bring goodness to an area of your body or your bubble, or you might just feel a gentle pulsation of energy or light around your body or your being. Remember, your natural energy defenses are fueled by love from the earth and guided by wisdom from your inner wisdom. As you allow these changes, you may see or feel the healing naturally grounding down into the earth and integrating with earth energies. When you are ready, you can allow the integrated earth energies to return to you and your bubble and then naturally extend out to the burgundy layer of your sphere of influence.

Now ask your inner wisdom to teach you and help you feel safe with and enjoy the burgundy layer of your sphere of influence. Allow your inner wisdom to readjust any outmoded beliefs or ways of being that no longer serve you. See, feel or experience this energy flow throughout your body, your genetic blueprint, your past, present, future, your mind and spiritual self. The energy then flows down to the earth, grounding the energy there, and the earth energy flows back up to fill your body and bubble with gentle, secure, soothing energy. As this energy emanates out from you, you see, feel or experience positive shifts and changes in your connections to the people, places and things in the burgundy layer.

Take a moment to feel gratitude for these energies, for the learning and for the healing. We now remember all that we have done, the place in nature, the layers of your sphere of influence with its burgundy outer layer. You remember syncing up with your inner wisdom and how you learned about your connections in the burgundy layer. You remember how easy it was to improve your connections to this layer by allowing change within yourself. You remember how you released obligations, rules, emotions, judgements about this layer. You remember grounding the learning and healing into the earth and receiving supportive earth energies that then healed or transformed your connections to the people, places or things within the burgundy layer of your sphere of influence. You also remember learning how to feel safe and enjoy this area and this part of your life.

Now it's time to come back to the room and back to your chair, back to your body and back to your current time and place. Feel your feet flat on the floor. Move your shoulders around. Move your toes. Move your fingers, and take a deep breath in and out. Slowly, in your own time, open your eyes.

Follow up questions

What people, places or things did you notice in the outer portion of your sphere of influence?

What insights, if any, did you receive about new ways of being with these people, places or things?

What part or parts were easy and what parts were hard

If you think about being safe with these people, places and things, how do you feel?

Did this help you feel safer? Please describe.

Exercise 5: Casual Acquaintances, Social Media & Coworkers

This part of your sphere of influence might feel a little closer to you. If you were to imagine it within the imagery of "orbits" of people, places or things, these "orbits" would be closer to you than your nation, local community or large associations. This is the category of people, places and things that you know, but not well. It might be a person you met at a party a time or two, a place you pass by but don't visit, or people you only know on social media or by passing them in the hall at work. While it may seem that these people, places or things are inconsequential, your relationship with them may be very impactful. For example, that person you met several times at a party seems nice and you like them, but also feel a sense of competition, judgement or jealousy between the two of you. Or, you often pass a church in your neighborhood and you feel guilty for not attending. Or, "friends" on social media try to smear their fear all over you. Or, you feel you need to dress to impress people at work who you hardly know. All of this can create a kind of pushing against you or a stress, and that interferes with your own authenticity and truth about who you are.

Grounding Meditation

Do this meditation seated in a chair, with your feet flat on the floor. If you like, you can lay down during the meditation, but if you find yourself falling asleep, you may choose to sit while doing these meditations. Always intend that your meditations be gentle, balanced and healthy for you. Please note that the following meditations include requests or intentions for learning and healing. You do not have to repeat each request or intention in full. Instead, when you read or hear the suggested intention or request, simply say to yourself, "Yes, I intend that."

Take a deep breath and close your eyes. Feel your body relax. With your imagination, see, feel or experience the bubble of light that surrounds you, your auric field. Your aura is a field of energy around you that contains all sorts of energies that help you live and thrive. You might see the aura has colors or shapes within it. Just take a moment to imagine floating in your energy field, with energies moving and flowing around you. Now, I invite you to see, feel or experience your whole aura to take on the color red, red like a beautiful ruby, but also filled with clear, lovely light. You see, feel or experience this red energy all the way around you. This red energy is the energy of vitality, health, excitement and thriving. Feel this red energy, and if you like, allow it to fill your entire body. Allow your body to match the vibration of this ruby red energy. The color of your energy field is now changing to orange, the bright, beautiful color of the inside of a sweet, ripe orange. This color has light and flow. Orange is the color of creativity, abundance, positive relationships and the preciousness of life. Allow your body to match this vibration and allow your body to drink in the orange light. The color changes again to yellow, the lemon color that brings confidence and empowerment, self-acceptance and integrity. It is the energy that says, yes I can! Allow this energy to swirl around you and fill you. Your entire being matches the vibration of this yellow energy. Now, the color changes to emerald green, the energy of healing and unconditional love. Let this energy surround you and fill you. Match this energy in every cell of your body. Again, the color changes, now to blue, like a vibrant blue sapphire. This light brings positive communication, authenticity and the ability to share your gifts with the world. You see, feel or experience this light around and within you. You become the blue, blue light. Now the light shifts to purple, the purple of amethyst. The amethyst light is in and around you, bringing intuition, intellectual insight and mental clarity. Finally, the light changes to white or gold. This golden or white light fills your aura and fills your body. It is your connection to the Divine. Feel the energy swirl or pulse through you. Take a moment to sit in this lovely energy. Now, come back to full awareness, take a deep breath, and open your eyes.

Imagery Meditation

Take a deep breath and close your eyes. Remember your auric field, the bubble of light that surrounds you. Feel the energies within this bubble. Notice that the outer edge of the bubble contains your natural energy defenses. See or experience or know that those defenses help you bring in the energies that are healthy and good and repel the unhealthy. You know at a deep level that your natural energy defenses are very responsive to your beliefs, thoughts, emotions and desires. The healthier those desires, thoughts, feelings and beliefs, the more your natural energy defenses can help you have healthy experiences with the energies coming in.

If you like, you can try that out. Think about something you love about yourself. If this is hard for you, pick something and pretend as if you loved it. It can be as small as loving your hair or as all encompassing as loving your soul. Focus your attention on that belief, say it to yourself like a mantra, do your best to feel the love, visualize it in some way. Now ask your inner wisdom to show you the love that is coming into your bubble that matches this belief in what you love about yourself and show you how your natural energy defenses help you in this. You might see the lovely white golden light on the outer edge of your bubble begin to form receptors or hooks or portals for this love to flow into your bubble. See it flow in or feel it flow in. Notice how good it feels to be both protected by your natural energy defenses and also receiving this love. Enjoy the love energy. It may feel as if you are drinking it in. Now take a moment to take stock and imagine all that you could do to work with your natural energy defenses to have the experiences you truly and deeply desire.

Now turn your attention to the area outside your bubble. This is your sphere of influence. You see the layers of your sphere of influence with its outer, deep burgundy color. The next closest layer is magenta, a bright red/pink color that is filled with energy.

The energy in this layer relates to people, places and things whose link to you is closer than the previous level, but not very personal. It relates to social media, people who you do not know well, things with a looser connection to you.

Ask your inner wisdom to teach you what you need to know about this magenta layer and your connections there. Allow this wisdom to flow throughout your whole being, your mind, your gut and emotions, your heart and out the front and back of your heart, to your present, future and past. Allow it to go into your soul and into the tiniest particles of you that make up your genetic blueprint and connect you to all of creation. Allow your inner wisdom to teach you in all of these parts of your consciousness what needs to change within you and how to allow and live with these changes. Allow your natural energy defenses to help and support you in this. Remember, your natural energy defenses are fueled by love that was created just for you. If you like, you can ask your inner wisdom to readjust any beliefs relating to the magenta layer of your sphere of influence. What you see, feel or experience with this magenta layer may change or shift in some way. Allow the transformation, allow the flow of wisdom and allow your natural energy defenses to work with balance and ease. You might notice that your natural energy defenses stay inside your bubble and the shifts in you naturally change the energies in the magenta layer. Allow yourself to see, feel or experience how changing your energy changes how you think, operate and feel in relation to the magenta layer of your sphere of influence. Now ground these energies of learning and transformation into the place where you connect to earth energies. Let the earth integrate and synthesize them. And allow the integrated energies back up to you and the bubble that surrounds you.

Now allow your natural energy defenses to heal any hurts, wounds, fears or unbalanced energy relating to this magenta layer. You may see, feel or experience energies speeding to a place within your body or within your bubble. Focus on the energies that surround that area. Notice that your natural energy defenses wrap around each part of you, and when you relax and allow, those natural energy defenses, bring balance and ease. You might notice that as you relax and allow, you can feel the love fueling your natural energy defenses. If you don't know how to relax, ask your inner wisdom to teach you how. Go ahead and see, feel or experience all of this healing flow down to the earth, integrate and synthesize and return to you and your bubble.

Now allow and intend your inner wisdom to teach you how to interact with this magenta layer in new and safe ways. If you like, you can ask to also learn how to interact with confidence or authenticity or joy or some other state that you desire. Allow this wisdom energy to permeate your whole being, throughout time and space, in all corners of your mind, spirit, heart, gut and emotions. See, feel or experience this energy flowing through the timeline of your being, through the tiny particles of your being and your whole body and soul. This energy carries a frequency. Simply allow yourself to match that frequency, receive its gifts and partner with this vibrant, enlightened part of yourself. Now ground all of this learning, all of these changes, all of the healing and all of the new ways of being down into the earth. See, feel or experience these energies going down through your body, out your feet and into the earth. They go down to where you connect to earth energies. You may see, feel or sense the wisdom energies mix and mingle with the earth energies, bringing integration, a deep sense of peace and a strong sense of potential. Allow this energy to now flow up from the earth to you and fill your body and your awareness and flow into and fill the bubble of energy around you.

Take a moment to feel gratitude for these energies, for the learning and for the healing. We now remember all that we have done. You remember how your natural energy defenses in the outer part of your bubble respond to your beliefs and help you receive the energies that match those beliefs. You remember how you can work with your natural energy defenses to emphasize the beliefs and experiences that you want most. You remember the layers within your sphere of influence and the magenta layer, relating to the loose connections of those people, places and things you may know. You remember syncing up with your inner wisdom and its teachings about how to interact with this layer. You remember how your natural energy defenses helped you heal as you learned and experienced relaxing into the healing and the love it brings to you. You remember learning from and partnering with your inner wisdom to create new ways of being with this magenta layer that allow you to be safe, secure and have the kinds of positive experiences you desire with this part of your life. You remember grounding the learning and healing into the earth itself and receiving supportive earth energies that filled your whole being.

Now it's time to come back to the room and back to your chair. Imagine your body and being in your body. Imagine your room and being in your room. Feel yourself seated in your chair in current time and space. Feel your feet flat on the floor. Move your shoulders around and take a deep breath in and out. Slowly, in your own time, open your eyes.

Follow up questions

What people, places or things are in the magenta layer of your sphere of influence?

What insights, if any, did you receive about new ways of being with these people, places or things?

How did it feel to relax into the healing and love from your natural energy defenses?

If you think about being safe with the people, places and things from the magenta layer, how do you feel?

Did this help you feel safer? Please describe.

Exercise 6: Close Coworkers, Close Neighbors, Family & Friends

This level of your sphere of influence is marked by those who learn and grow with you, or whose resistance to growth brings opportunities for deepening your personal understandings about yourself and life. These connections may be very rewarding, bringing fun, adventure, support, creativity, companionship, love and more. These connections may also bring unconscious restrictions, preconditions or "strings attached," hurtful judgements, conflicts or other energetic complications that suck the joy out of this sphere of influence. If you don't have coworkers or close neighbors, think of customers, clients, patients, students, teachers or members of any group with whom you share thoughts, feelings or a sense of personal connection. All of the people within this sphere give you attention. The purpose of the following exercises is to help you improve the quality of that attention and the shared intellectual, creative and emotional energies that may be exchanged. This may also relate to things, places or concepts that connect to you in meaningful ways, that might be your home, a physical area or something like your work or profession or hobbies. All of these might feel quite personal to you. And it may be surprising how much we all have to learn about this area within our own sphere of influence.

Grounding Meditation

Do this meditation seated in a chair, with your feet flat on the floor. If you like, you can lay down during the meditation, but if you find yourself falling asleep, you may choose to sit while doing these meditations. Always intend that your meditations be gentle, balanced and healthy for you. Please note that the following meditations include requests or intentions for learning and healing. You do not have to repeat each request or intention in full. Instead, when you read or hear the suggested intention or request, simply say to yourself, "Yes, I intend that."

Take a deep breath and close your eyes. Feel your body relax. With your imagination, see, feel or experience the bubble of light that surrounds you, your auric field. Your aura is a field of energy around you that contains all sorts of energies that help you live and thrive. You might see the aura has colors or shapes within it. Just take a moment to imagine sitting in your chair, with energies of your aura moving and flowing around you. Now imagine that a cord or beam of light or energy drops down from your feet or tailbone, down through your bubble, down through the floor and building and into the earth. This cord drops down to that place where you connect to the earth. You might see this place as a sphere, a crystal, a room, a cave or some other space. Notice that a part of your consciousness is always there, immersed in the peaceful, clean, clear energies of the earth. The cord of light from your feet or tailbone comes down to this space and connects. It might plug in, hook on or meld in some other way. With this connection, you can easily feel the pure, clean energies of the earth. And, you begin to sense the heartbeat of the earth reverberate up the cord and into your bubble and into your body. You feel that calm, strong rhythmic beat vibrating up the cord. You find that your body and your senses begin to match that beat, begin to pulse with the same rhythm. Notice how the rhythm calms you, soothes you and brings you into your natural sense of clarity and wellbeing. Take a moment to sit in this lovely energy. Now, come back to full awareness, take a deep breath, and open your eyes.

Imagery Meditation

Close your eyes, focus on your breath, reconnect with that feeling or knowing of the earth's heartbeat and your connection to it and your experience with it. Now turn your attention to your sphere of influence. We have explored the burgundy and magenta layers. Now focus on the next inner layer. You might see this as a true red color or even a red orange. Reconnect with the flow of wisdom from your inner wisdom. You remember what it felt like to receive the flow of wisdom from the crystal at the top of the spire. Reconnect with this flow, ask your inner wisdom to share with you the best kinds of energies, beliefs, experiences, emotions and healing or growth possible for you within this layer and anything else you need to know about your relation to this layer. See, feel or experience this wisdom coming to you, filling you up. It goes into every corner of your mind, your body and your soul. It goes into your cells, your genetic material and every particle of your being. It goes out the back of your heart to your past and out the front of your heart to your future and in all directions to the present and to parts of your consciousness that are outside the flow of time. It flows down through your body, into the earth, to your place of connection to the earth. You might see, feel or experience the energy of wisdom mix, mingle and integrate there. Now it flows back up your grounding cord, into your body, filling your body, flowing out the top of your head and filling the bubble that surrounds you.

Now intend that your inner wisdom and your natural energy defenses team up to release old fears, pains, traumas, negative beliefs or any other energetic debris that block your optimal experience of this area of your sphere of influence. You may experience in some way that your natural defenses are being enriched with wisdom and, in turn, are suffusing your body and being with energy, support and wisdom. You may also experience your natural energy defenses begin to interact with any mental, emotional or spiritual blocks to your happiness in this area. Allow yourself to experience, see imagery, feel sensations, have knowings or even just pretend as if positive changes are being made within you that help you to your goal of ease, happiness and security in this part of your life.

If you like, you can give permission to your natural energy defenses to remove any oaths, obligations or agreements you have made that block your happiness in this area. If you feel that you need permission to be happy in this part of your life, ask your inner wisdom or, if you like, your higher power to give you that permission. See the healing and the permission as light or energy that flow to you and fill you up, making changes and going to all aspects of your being. Stay in the place of allowing and observe by visualizing, feeling or experiencing these flows of energy. Remember, your natural energy defenses are fueled by love. You notice that there is more than enough power, more than enough wisdom and more than enough time for these processes to balance your system, bring you wisdom and support your happiness and safety in this area of your life. You may see, feel or experience how the changes to you naturally changes the appearance, feeling or experience of that red layer of your sphere of influence. As the quality of the energy within you improves, the quality of the energy you experience with this layer changes for the better.

Now allow all of this learning, healing and growth to flow down through your body, down through your feet, down into the earth. You see, feel or experience this energy speed down to that place deep within the earth that secures your experience of what it means for you to live on the earth, in your life and in your own being. All of these energies integrate, synthesize and create a new sense of security and truth for you. That security and truth and integration flows upward. It comes up through the layers of the earth, up through the floor and into your feet. It flows all the way up through your body and out the top of your head, filling your whole body, your whole mind, your whole being and your whole energy field, surrounding you, 360 degrees around you, beneath your feet and above your head. You are filled and surrounded by the integrated energy of transformation.

Next, ask your inner wisdom to teach you through a flow of energy how to experience and live with this transformation and your new perspectives and experiences with the bright red layer of your sphere of influence. Again, you see, feel and experience the flow of wisdom fill all of the areas of your being, your mind, body, soul and emotions, your past, present, future and all of your genetic material. It goes beyond time, and it flows down to the earth to integrate there and back up to you, filling your body and the bubble that surrounds you.

Take a moment to feel gratitude for these energies, for the learning and for the healing. We now remember all that we have done. You remember the red layer of your sphere of influence and how your inner wisdom taught you about the best possible experiences you can have with this part of your sphere of influence. You remember releasing old fears, traumas and pains as well as oaths, obligations or agreements that block these optimal experiences. You remember receiving permission to experience the happiness and safety that is possible for you in this area of your sphere of influence. You remember learning how to create and maintain these optimal experiences. You remember grounding, integrating and synthesizing the learning and healing into the earth itself, and you remember receiving supportive earth energies that filled your whole being and the bubble that surrounds you.

Now it's time to come back to the room and back to your chair. Imagine your body and being in your body. Imagine your room and being in your room. Feel yourself seated in your chair in current time and space. Feel your feet flat on the floor. Move your shoulders around and take a deep breath in and out. Slowly, in your own time, open your eyes.

Follow up questions

What are the optimal experiences relating to the red layer of your sphere of influence?

What insights, if any, did you receive about new ways of being with these people, places or things?

What part or parts were easy and what parts were hard?

If you think about being safe with these people, places and things, how do you feel?

Did this help you feel safer? Please describe.

Exercise 7: Close Family and Close Friends and Lovers

These are the people, places and things that you feel strongly with your heart. They may impact your identity and they may wield strong influences on your beliefs and perspectives. These are potentially some of the most rewarding or devastating connections in life. For some, religion, professional success or physical objects may also fall into this category. Many people would say that their significant other is in his or her own orbit. While this may be true, for the purposes of this exercise we will group all of these types of connections together.

Grounding Meditation

Do this meditation seated in a chair, with your feet flat on the floor. If you like, you can lay down during the meditation, but if you find yourself falling asleep, you may choose to sit while doing these meditations. Always intend that your meditations be gentle, balanced and healthy for you. Please note that the following meditations include requests or intentions for learning and healing. You do not have to repeat each request or intention in full. Instead, when you read or hear the suggested intention or request, simply say to yourself, "Yes, I intend that."

Take a deep breath and close your eyes. Feel your body relax. With your imagination, see, feel or experience the bubble of light that surrounds you, your auric field. Just take a moment to check in with the energies of your aura moving and flowing around you. Now see, feel or experience how the bubble that surrounds you is deeply connected to your heart. You might see something like a funnel in front and in back of your heart that breathes energy from your bubble in and out. Imagine breathing energy from your bubble into your heart and back out to your bubble. Now, imagine lines of energy from your feet and hands, connecting your bubble to your heart. You might experience beautiful, bright particles of light that move from your aura into your heart and touch it deeply. Allow yourself to see, feel or experience how your heart and aura connect and communicate. Take a moment to sit in this lovely energy. Now, come back to full awareness, take a deep breath, and open your eyes.

Imagery Meditation

Again, you are sitting down, relaxed, and you close your eyes. Breathing slowly and deeply, you focus on your breath. You visualize it coming in through your nose, into your sinuses and down your throat. The breath goes down into the top of your lungs, the middle of your lungs and deep into your lungs. And you breathe out. As you breathe in again, you let the breath into your whole lungs, and then you see the breath move into your heart. The heart is given life by this breath and the breath out releases stagnation. Take a few more breaths into and out of your heart. And now move your attention to the bubble that surrounds you. See, feel or experience how your breath and the connection of your bubble to your heart becomes synchronized, partnered, a part of a bigger dynamic as you focus on your breath. Switch your attention to the energies in your bubble that represent beliefs, ideas and perspectives. Imagine or pretend as if a positive belief, such as "I am loveable" lives inside your bubble in the form of energy. See, feel or experience that the energy of your positive belief begins to move from your aura into your heart. If that movement is blocked in any way, ask your natural energy defenses to remove those blocks and support you by integrating your positive belief into your heart.

If you like, you can ask your inner wisdom to teach your natural energy defenses how to remove these blocks in the most effective, safe and easy ways. You can see, feel or experience this wisdom flowing through every part of you, all of time and even to your consciousness that does not experience time. You ground this knowing into the earth and let the integrated energy return to you and fill your bubble. As your bubble is filled with the integrated, synthesized earth energies, you may experience added ease in connecting your positive belief with your heart.

You may experience new and pleasant energies begin to trickle or flow into your heart. If, on the other hand, you experience discomfort, ask your natural energy defenses to release any pain, fear, trauma or other dysfunction that prevents you from experiencing the joy and goodness of your positive belief. Notice that some of these difficult energies might belong to other people. Watch as your natural energy defenses find the energies that do not belong to you and release them. Also notice how your natural energy defenses easily processes and releases your own energies of negative thoughts and emotions.

If you feel that your heart is filled with the consciousness of other people, places or things, and there is no room for your own beliefs or your own consciousness, ask your inner wisdom to teach you how to live with your consciousness, your beliefs, your unique being centered within your heart. Again, you let this learning into every part of your body, mind, emotions, genetic material, and experience of time and no time as well as your soul. You ground the energy, allowing the earth to integrate it deeply and then let that integrated energy return to your body, your being and the bubble that surrounds you. Notice that as your natural energy defenses interact with all of these energies, you simply watch, observe and allow.

If you find yourself trying to push the energy or use your will, turn your attention to your breath and find that place of allowing, letting your natural energy defenses do the work. Remember, these defenses are fueled by love for you, easily flowing into your system from the earth. There is more than enough power, more than enough ability of your defenses to cleanse and balance you. And of course, if you have any oaths, obligations or promises that interfere with this cleansing, balancing process, you can ask your natural energy defense system to release and dissolve them. Now, return to your positive belief. Allow it to touch your heart, to interact with your heart and fill your heart.

Now, expand your awareness out to your sphere of influence. You have seen the burgundy, magenta, and true red layers and you now see the next inner layer as the color orange, bright and beautiful orange. Ask your inner wisdom to teach you anything you need to know about this orange layer of your sphere of influence. Allow the energy of this wisdom to fill all of you, all of time and no time, your soul, your mind, your emotions and your physicality, even your genetic blueprint. It now grounds into the earth and connects to earth energies where the wisdom, the earth and your own being are harmonized. Allow the harmonious energy to return to you, filling you and your bubble.

Allow your natural energy defenses to cleanse you, your bubble and your heart of any energies that give you pain, discomfort or fear. You watch all blockages disappear as well as energies that do not belong to you. Ground these healing energies where they harmonize and integrate and allow the harmonized, integrated energies to return to you and the bubble that surrounds you.

Now ask your inner wisdom to teach you anything else you need to know to feel safe and joyful, healthy and balanced with this orange layer of your sphere of influence. You allow the wisdom energy into your whole being, you ground the energy into the earth and you let it come back to you, filling you and your bubble.

Now, return to your heart. See, feel or experience the energy of your positive belief still deep within your heart. Express this truth from your heart to the orange layer by saying with your heart, "This is me." As you communicate through your heart to this orange layer, you might imagine that the energy of the belief is flowing out your heart to your bubble. Your bubble then emanates this truth out in all directions. It sounds out, like a beautiful tone and the orange layer receives this sound and is enhanced. The orange layer tones back, in perhaps a matching or harmonious frequency. As your bubble absorbs the incoming frequency, allow yourself to experience the energies. If this is difficult for you, allow your natural energy defenses to help you feel safe in this. If you feel overwhelmed, ask your inner wisdom to teach you how to cope with the goodness, love, ease and safety of these energies.

Take a moment to enjoy and feel gratitude for these energies. We now remember all that we have done. You remember the breaths from your heart to your aura and how your heart and aura connect and communicate. You remember picking a positive belief and letting the energy of that belief flow from your aura to your heart. You remember all of the healing and learning around this communication. You remember learning how to live with your consciousness or being filling your heart. You remember the positive belief touching your heart and perhaps filling your heart. You remember learning how to be safe and easy with the orange layer of your sphere of influence, all the healing and all the growth. And you remember allowing the energies of your positive belief out of your heart to your bubble and the sound or frequency that emanated out of your bubble to the orange layer and the corresponding frequency that returned to you. You remember how that felt and how you were able to accept all the goodness meant for you.

Now it's time to come back to the room and back to your chair. Imagine your body and being in your body. Imagine your room and being in your room. Feel yourself seated in your chair in your current time and space. Feel your feet flat on the floor. Move your shoulders around and take a deep breath. Slowly, in your own time, open your eyes.

Follow up questions

How did your heart feel as you breathed into it and as you allowed it to connect to the positive belief?

What was your positive belief and how do you feel about it now?

Do you feel your own consciousness in your heart? Do you need to make changes that will allow you to feel this more fully?

Do you feel that your positive belief is a part of your authentic self? If not, is there anything you need to do to better integrate that into your understanding of the real you?

What did it feel like to receive the frequency from the orange layer of your sphere of influence?

Did this help you feel safer? Please describe.

Exercise 8: Self

This is you, inside your auric field, the bubble of light that surrounds you. As you have seen in the previous exercises, your natural energy defenses interact with your self by dissolving negative beliefs, cleansing your system of old emotions, memories or energies that no longer serve you and fostering healthy energetic environments to grow new, productive beliefs, guided by your highest wisdom. In the following section, we will explore your ability to be and live from your authentic self.

Grounding Meditation

Do this meditation seated in a chair, with your feet flat on the floor. If you like, you can lay down during the meditation, but if you find yourself falling asleep, you may choose to sit while doing these meditations. Always intend that your meditations be gentle, balanced and healthy for you. Please note that the following meditations include requests or intentions for learning and healing. You do not have to repeat each request or intention in full. Instead, when you read or hear the suggested intention or request, simply say to yourself, "Yes, I intend that."

Take a deep breath and close your eyes. Feel your body relax. Feel all the sensations in your body. Feel the areas of relaxation and the areas of tension. Simply observe. If you are sensitive to the flow of energy, you may feel energies flowing through your body or energies flowing to you. Put your focus on your skin. Allow yourself to feel any sensations of your skin. Perhaps you feel the temperature of the air or the compression of your backside into the chair. Expand your awareness to all of the skin of your body. Sense it as a whole system. Notice how it covers your whole body from your armpits to your toe tips to the circumference of your scalp. Feel the wholeness that your skin brings to your system. Enjoy this wholeness for a moment. Now, come back to full awareness, take a deep breath, and open your eyes.

Imagery Meditation

Close your eyes, focus on your breath, reconnect with the sensation of your skin. Now imagine the aura or bubble that surrounds you. See, feel or experience the vital, bright energies that are all around you. Turn your attention to your body and its skin. If you see or sense any dark energies or energies that don't belong, ask your natural energy defenses to remove them. They easily lift or peel off of you and float away, up to the universe or down to the earth to be transformed. Your natural energy defenses then fill the space with love. Allow and watch the love fill up that space. Now, your natural energy defenses begin to vacuum away any unneeded, unhelpful energies. Take some time to watch or feel your energetic skin become clean and rejuvenated. You may see or sense other layers under your skin that represent your burdens or worries. Allow your natural energy defenses to peel these layers off, one by one, releasing them to float away or sink away, out of your awareness, or vacuum all of the layers away. Keep allowing each layer to be cleansed and rejuvenated, until you get down to your core self. This may look or seem like your body is made of light or a ball of light or some other object or symbol. It may be bright and glowing or your core self might need cleansing and healing from your natural energy defenses. Just allow your natural energy defenses and the vacuum to help you release all of the uncomfortable energy and rejuvenate everything with love. When you can see, feel or experience the bright core that is left, step into that brightness and become it. Melt into it. You may experience flows of energies, or a deeper sense of relaxation or a wonderful stillness that is pregnant with possibilities and the vitality to fulfill them. Or you might just feel love or loved. If you like, from this place of brightness, say, "I experience my being."

Now shift your awareness so that you can look down toward the earth. See that your core self has roots that extend down into the earth, allowing you to receive love, vitality and life from the earth. Make the intention that your natural energy defenses protect these roots, knowing that the roots feed love to your natural energy defenses and that your natural energy defenses maintain a vibration of love energy around these roots. Anything that is less than love cannot sync up or connect in any way.

Now, become aware of your body, with its glowing center, glowing roots extending to the earth and all the love protection around the roots, around your center and around your body. If you like, make the intention, "I intend my natural energy defenses to surround my center, roots and body and being with love and protection." See, feel or experience allowing your natural energy defenses to implement this intention. Allow the love energy to come up your roots and power your natural energy defenses.

Turn your attention to your inner wisdom and ask it to teach you what you need to know about your core self and how to feel safe and secure in your core. Now, see, feel or experience the energy of wisdom flowing to you. It goes into every cell of your body, every molecule, and every gene. It goes into every corner of your mind, your heart and your gut and deeply into your heart, where your soul resides. It flows backwards behind you, as if it is filling the timeline of your life, all of your lives and all of the connections throughout time that form your thoughts, awareness and consciousness. And this light flows forward in front of you into all of your hopes, dreams, intentions and beliefs and all of the connections that will form your thoughts, awareness and consciousness. It goes to your present and it goes beyond time. Now intend the wisdom energy to flow down through your body, down through your feet, down into the earth to the place where you connect to the earth. The wisdom flows there and integrates and synthesizes with the earth energies. Allow this harmonized, integrated energy to flow up from the earth to you and fill your body and the bubble that surrounds you.

Now, ask your natural energy defenses to release and dissolve any connection or attachment you have to past pain, fear, trauma or other discomfort in relation to your core self. Now see, feel or experience your natural energy defenses go to the places where you experience physical pain, emotional pain, spiritual pain or psychic pain about yourself. As these pains or memories of pain release and lift away, they flow up, out and away or down to the earth to be transformed into something better. You watch, feel or experience the healing flow into your psychic senses, clearing them of pain. This might be through your eyes, ears, nose, mouth, hands, feet, heart, gut or any other part of you that relates to your psychic senses. You see, feel or experience the healing energy flow deep, deep, deep into your heart, releasing emotional pain, and deeper still into your soul, releasing pain or dysfunction there. The light flows out the back of your heart throughout all the connections you have with the past. The pains or wounds there lift and float away. When that is complete, you see, feel or experience the light flow out the front of your heart to your connections to the future you. All the pains and all the fears of pain release and float away. The healing goes to your whole heart, to your present and to the unconscious experiences of no time, like sleep, releasing pain and dysfunction from these areas in ways that are easy and gentle. And you ground this healing into the earth where the healing is integrated into your life. This integrated energy returns to you, filling you and the bubble that surrounds you.

Now ask your inner wisdom to teach you how to live from your core self in ways that are safe and fulfilling and joyful. See, feel or experience the wisdom energy flowing all around you, feeding your core with light and goodness, wisdom and a deep knowing that allows you to easily live from this true place from within yourself. Notice that this is a place of being more than a place of doing. Now allow the energy to flow from your core down to the earth, grounding there and then back up to your body and then up out of your head and shower all around you.

Take a moment to relax and enjoy the experience of your empowered core self. We now remember all that we have done. You remember the release of all the layers of dark energies around you and how you found your bright core within. You remember the glowing roots into the earth and how your natural energy defenses protect your roots as well as your core. You remember learning about your core, releasing past pains or dysfunctions and allowing your core to become more empowered so that you can live your best and most authentic life.

Now it's time to come back to the room and back to your chair. Imagine your body and being in your body. Imagine your room and being in your room. Feel yourself seated in your chair in your current time and space. Feel your feet flat on the floor. Move your shoulders around and take a deep breath. Slowly, in your own time, open your eyes.

Follow up questions

What did you experience when you connected to your core?

What insights, if any, did you receive about your core or about being centered?

What part or parts were easy and what parts were hard?

Do you have a new understanding of your authentic self or how to live more authentically?

Did this help you feel safer? Please describe.

Exercise 9: Resistance # 1

Resistance is just fear based beliefs and emotions that block health and wellbeing. For example, let's say you scratch yourself and it bleeds a little bit. If you begin to worry with lots of emotion that it may never heal, that you will get an infection, that you got scratched because you are an inferior human being or that it's another reason why you hate your life, you will block the healing. Studies of the placebo and nocebo effect have shown that thoughts and beliefs matter to health and wellbeing. Now think about negative beliefs that may be living in your subconscious. These beliefs are recorded and are set into play without your conscious awareness. It's just a knee jerk reaction to think and feel a certain way under certain conditions. Think of Pavlov's dog who salivates at the ring of a bell, even if there is no food in sight. Our lives work in this way. We experience something that reminds us of something else and we unconsciously react. This reaction is so fast that our conscious mind cannot possibly keep up. The trick is to access and change those unconscious beliefs, learn new beliefs and ways of being and ground them into our reality.

Let's do that now.

Grounding Meditation

Do this meditation seated in a chair, with your feet flat on the floor. If you like, you can lay down during the meditation, but if you find yourself falling asleep, you may choose to sit while doing these meditations. Always intend that your meditations be gentle, balanced and healthy for you. Please note that the following meditations include requests or intentions for learning and healing. You do not have to repeat each request or intention in full. Instead, when you read or hear the suggested intention or request, simply say to yourself, "Yes, I intend that."

Take a deep breath and close your eyes. Your body relaxes easily. You know how to let the muscles of your legs relax and allow them to be heavy. You feel your feet resting on the floor, feeling the long bones in your feet, the metatarsals, widen and expand. Your toes uncurl. Your heels soften. Your ankles release. Your knees can rest. As you move your attention to your tailbone, it straightens, balanced between left and right, front and back. You might feel a pleasant warmth at the top of your thigh bones, the femurs, right where they connect to your hips and glutes. It's as if the warm, pleasant feeling radiates out to the muscles and begins to sync up with the pulse of your tailbone. Your tailbone and your hip bones also feel that pulse. Notice your pelvic bones sync up to this rhythm. It's as if a metronome is thrumming through your lower body. It may begin to feel as if this tempo is the same tempo as the earth. You are you and the earth is the earth, but you are both pulsing to the same rhythm. This rhythm rises up through your body. You may experience several different rhythms in your midsection, but as you focus on the rhythm in your lower body, your torso catches that rhythm and syncs up. This is enhanced and speeded by you relaxing your muscles, allowing the tempo to spread upward. Now you allow your shoulders to relax. Now, your arms, elbows, wrists and hands. Your fingers are pulsing to the rhythm. Now your voice box is pulsing to the rhythm. Your throat, neck muscles and spine join in. Now your face syncs up. Your scalp syncs up, and your brain syncs up. The whole of you is easily, restfully pulsing to this same, steady rhythm. Take a moment to enjoy the rhythm. Now, come back to full awareness, take a deep breath, and open your eyes.

Imagery Meditation

Close your eyes, relax your body and return to the image and sensations of being in rhythm with the beat of the earth. Now begin to scan your body. Imagine that you could see inside of your body and begin to see that under your skin is a fine membrane of energy. It wraps your body with energy, and if you were to look further, you would see that this membrane wraps everything in your body, every muscle, every bone, every organ. It wraps your brain, your nerves and your veins. It wraps the smallest bits of you and the largest bits of you. Your natural energy defenses work within these membranes. Now expand your awareness to the bubble that surrounds you. It too is surrounded by an energy membrane. If you look closely at this membrane at the edge of your bubble, you would see that it is actually made up of a web of connections, intersecting and connecting to make a strong energy barrier that can allow in the good and keep out the bad. As you continue to examine your bubble, you see that the web extends throughout your bubble, creating pathways and connections that allow beautiful positive energy to flow to your body and to your consciousness. Watch how your natural energy defenses work within these webs, bringing love energy to these spaces, pumping goodness to all of you, your whole body and the whole bubble that surrounds you. You might feel the rhythm of the earth energy ripple through these web-like energy structures. Allow yourself to notice what this feels like.

As you scan your body and your bubble, you might see areas that need healing. Perhaps an area needs to be closed up or smoothed out or carries some dense energies. If you like, you can ask your highest wisdom to teach your natural energy defenses how to make these areas whole. Remember the flow of wisdom, how it surrounds you and fills you, going to your whole mind, heart and gut, going to all the cells and genetic materials in your body. It goes to your heart and out the front and back of your heart, to your present and to your soul, and it grounds down into the earth where this knowledge is integrated and synthesized. The integrated energy comes back up from the earth to you, filling you up and spilling out to fill the bubble that surrounds you. Now see, feel or experience how your natural energy defenses heal and make whole all of these membranes inside your body and in the field of energy that surrounds you. Simply allow that wholeness to form. It is a natural process like digestion or the healing of your skin.

Now ask your inner wisdom to teach you how to release any beliefs or other energies that block your health and wellbeing and with them, remove any trauma, pain, fear or any emotion that is connected to your blocks. As before, you watch and experience the wisdom flow through all the parts of you, including your past, present, future and genetic structures. You allow the wisdom to ground down to the earth and the synthesized energy to fill your body and the bubble that surrounds you. As you watch or experience this flow of wisdom you might see, feel or experience emotions or energies release up, out and away.

Finally, ask your inner wisdom to teach you and help you understand anything else you need to know in order to easily and gently partner with your natural energy defenses and allow them to help you thrive and create happiness in your life. Visualize the wisdom filling up the tiniest bits of you and the whole of you, the whole timeline of your life, the whole breadth of your mind, the entirety of your gut and soul and you ground this wisdom and receive and allow the integrated energy to fill you, through your body, to and throughout your bubble.

It's time now to come back to your room and back to your chair, but before you do, let's remember all that you have done. You remember seeing the membranes within and around your body, seeing how your natural energy defenses permeate your whole being and the bubble that surrounds you. You remember the healing of any area of need within this system of membranes, and you remember the learning you received from your inner wisdom about how to heal, how to release the beliefs that created blockages for you and how to partner with your natural energy defenses so that you can allow them to support you in thriving and creating happiness and goodness in your life.

Now it's time to come back to the room and back to your chair. Imagine your body and being in your body. Imagine your room and being in your room. Feel yourself seated in your chair in your current time and space. Feel your feet flat on the floor. Move your shoulders around and take a deep breath in and out. Slowly, in your own time, open your eyes.

Follow up questions

What does it feel like to be surrounded and permeated by your natural energy defenses?

What insights, if any, did you receive about your resistance?

What part or parts were easy and what parts were hard?

Are there areas within your bubble or your energy system that need more healing? Please describe.

Did this help you feel safer? Please describe.

Exercise 10: Resistance #2

This exercise is for those who feel blocked or unsure of their connection to their inner wisdom. The purpose of this exercise is to connect your inner wisdom to your higher power in a way that allows you to access the highest wisdom possible for your growth and happiness. Sometimes, we allow our wisdom to be clouded by the influences of other people or energies that are not directed in our best interest. This exercise will help clear this. If you do not believe in a higher power, you may want to take some time to ponder how you want your mind to be influenced or guided. Whether we like it or not, our minds are greatly influenced by the thoughts, energies and intentions of others. I believe that you deserve to be informed by your highest source of wisdom. You get to choose what that is. During this exercise, tailor your experience of your higher power in a way that works best for you.

Grounding Meditation

Do this meditation seated in a chair, with your feet flat on the floor. If you like, you can lay down during the meditation, but if you find yourself falling asleep, you may choose to sit while doing these meditations. Always intend that your meditations be gentle, balanced and healthy for you. Please note that the following meditations include requests or intentions for learning and healing. You do not have to repeat each request or intention in full. Instead, when you read or hear the suggested intention or request, simply say to yourself, "Yes, I intend that."

Take a deep breath and close your eyes. Take a moment and remember our first exercise with its beautiful place in nature, the walk and the house or castle with its spire. Go back to that place. Feel the nature all around you. Enjoy the beautiful day. Feel the earth beneath your feet. Feel your connection to the earth there. Extend your awareness into the earth and find that place where you connect to your understanding about what it means to live on the earth, and in the universe and in your own being. That place may feel very secure, homelike, or just full of energy. Don't worry if you can't clearly connect, just pretend as if you could experience a place deep within the earth that cleanses and synthesizes energies, that helps you feel secure and grounded, that brings you balance and vitality. Now, remember your connection to your inner wisdom through the crystal at the top of the spire. Allow yourself to realize that you don't need to be in the spire to access that wisdom or feel that flow of wisdom from the crystal. Just intend that your inner wisdom is connected to and informed by your higher power. If you like, you can state that as an intention. Just state the name of your higher power and say, "I intend that my inner wisdom is connected to and informed by you in ways that are healthy and balanced for me." Allow yourself to experience that connection. If this is difficult for you, pretend as if you are experiencing this connection. Say to yourself, "If I had such a balanced and healthy connection, what would it feel like?" Take a moment to sit in the flow of this energy and connection. Now, come back to full awareness, take a deep breath, and open your eyes.

Imagery Meditation

Close your eyes, focus on your breath, reconnect with your experience of connection to both the earth and your inner wisdom with its link to your higher power. Allow yourself to feel those connections. You may see or experience a flow of energy. This should feel healthy and balanced, positive and safe. Now make the intention to your higher power, "Heal my connections and transform any of my beliefs or perspectives I hold that block the healthy flow of learning, information or assistance from my higher power to my inner wisdom and my being so that the flow of learning, information and assistance is healthy, balanced and supports my health and wellbeing." See, feel or experience this energy flow to you, through you and around you. It might come in through your head, in through your feet or in through your bubble. It goes into every corner of your mind, your heart and your gut. It goes deeply into your spirit or soul. It permeates all of your genetic material. It goes out the back of your heart to your past, permeating your past. It goes out the front of your heart to your future. It permeates your future. It goes to your present, filling it completely. Now allow this energy to flow down to the earth to that place that integrates and synthesizes energies for you. Allow the earth to do its part in integrating these energies for you. And now allow the earth energies to flow up, into your body and out into the field of energy that surrounds you.

Return your attention to the flow of energy from your inner wisdom and its balanced link to your higher power. Name your higher power and make this intention, "Teach and help my natural energy defenses to release any trauma, pain, fear, difficult emotion or dysfunction that relates to my inner wisdom and its connection to you." Now allow that energy of teaching and assistance to flow through every part of you, ground down into the earth and return to you and the bubble of energy that surrounds you.

Again, turn your attention to your inner wisdom and its link to your higher power. Name your higher power and make the intention, "Teach my natural energy defenses to dissolve, resolve and release any attachments to false wisdom that I may have mistakenly accepted and teach me how to know the difference between the energy of my inner wisdom and false wisdom." Allow this healing and teaching to flow to every part of you throughout time. You may see, feel or experience a release of influence from advertisements, pundits, all types of media, gurus, teachers, loved ones or oppressors. You may be released from spiritual energies that cannot access your higher power and its truth. You may experience emotions, beliefs or ways of being release from you. You may experience new ways of working with your mind or intellect or the feeling, perhaps for the first time, that you have the right to choose your thoughts and how they are guided. You may feel as if your free will is being empowered and cleansed so that you can experience both freedom and loyalty to your own truth. You may experience old agreements, permissions or mistakes dissolve and disappear. Now allow all of this learning and healing to flow down to the earth, integrate and synthesize and return to you, filling you and the energy bubble that surrounds you.

Take a moment to enjoy these flows of energies and let them come to a place of balance. Now it's time to return to your room and return to your chair, but before you do, let's remember all that you have done. You remember your connection to the earth and your inner wisdom, informed by your higher power. You remember clearing old unhealthy beliefs about your connection to your higher power. You remember releasing trauma, pain and dysfunction about this connection and you remember how your natural energy defenses learned more about releasing these old burdens. You remember letting go of false wisdom and any connections, mistakes or agreements to false wisdom, allowing your free will to shine and be healed and empowered by the truth and health of your higher power. And you remember how the earth took in all of these energies and integrated them in such a way that you could own them and live them.

Now it's time to come back to the room and back to your chair. Take a deep breath. Move your fingers and toes. Feel yourself in your chair and when you are ready, open your eyes.

Follow up questions

What are your thoughts and feelings about being connected to a higher power?

If the idea of a higher power repels you, can you come up with some other positive metaphor that puts you into a flow of higher truth rather than false wisdom? If so, what is it?

What part or parts were easy and what parts were hard?

After doing this meditation, how do you feel about your own will? Do you need to make different choices in order to keep it from being contaminated by the unhealthy intentions of others?

Did this help you feel safer? Please describe.

Exercise 11: Resistance #3

If you feel generally blocked or that, at a deep level, you need to rinse off or detach from energies, emotions or thoughts but have not yet found a way to make that happen, this exercise might help. During this exercise, you will use a "light touch" when focusing your intention and expectation. This is helpful for those who are practicing the law of attraction as it teaches how to work with the unconscious without overwhelming it. Also, keep in mind that your subconscious is a part of you. It is not an outside force that is trying to trip you up. It is a valuable, worthy and precious part of you.

Grounding Meditation

Do this meditation seated in a chair, with your feet flat on the floor. If you like, you can lay down during the meditation, but if you find yourself falling asleep, you may choose to sit while doing these meditations. Always intend that your meditations be gentle, balanced and healthy for you. Please note that the following meditations include requests or intentions for learning and healing. You do not have to repeat each request or intention in full. Instead, when you read or hear the suggested intention or request, simply say to yourself, "Yes, I intend that."

Take a deep breath and close your eyes. Allow your body to relax. You might feel your feet or hands relax or the muscles in the back of your neck soften. You feel your slow, deep breaths and you might even feel your heart beating. Now turn your attention inward. Imagine that your conscious awareness is in a kind of gentle quicksand and that it begins to sink down from your head. It goes down past your eyes, down past your face, down past your neck and throat and into your torso. Intend that your awareness goes to where your subconscious lives. This may be in a part of your body where you see a shape, color or symbol that represents your subconscious. Others may feel their awareness move farther inward as if your conscious mind could travel to deeper and different dimensions within yourself. You might imagine that you have layers of consciousness, and you are traveling to the layer that is in great need of goodness, gentleness and healing. Know that this part of your subconscious is so, so worthy of so, so much goodness, even if it is resisting goodness. Once you arrive at this level of the subconscious, or if you see or experience the subconscious within the body, just sit with it. Be with it. Your presence is very healing to it. Your attention alone brings goodness. If you are feeling judgement or fear for this part of yourself, turn your attention to simply allowing yourself to be in this space with your subconscious. What you see or experience might change, or it might not. You may experience the release of emotions or thoughts or memories. Now, with deep respect, thank your subconscious for letting you spend time with it and promise it that you will return again very soon. Take a deep breath, come back to your awareness of your body and open your eyes.

Imagery Meditation

Take a breath and close your eyes. Now, return to that feeling of relaxation, sinking down from your head and into your body. Also, remember your connection to the flow of learning from your inner wisdom. Once you experience that connection, ask your inner wisdom how to best work with your subconscious in ways that are gentle, kind, respectful and effective. And ask your inner wisdom to teach your subconscious how to accept and safely experience goodness, how to trust in its worthiness of goodness and how to trust itself. Allow that learning into every part of you, your mind, heart and gut. It goes to the whole of your past, and the whole of your future and the whole of your present. It goes to the whole of your genetics and physical being and the whole of your soul. And this knowledge grounds down through your body and into the earth, down to that place where you connect to the earth, where this knowledge is integrated and synthesized. Imagine that the earth is actually helping you claim and own this information so that you can live it with ease. All you need to do is allow the earth to do its part. You may continue to experience a flow of learning energy as you allow the earth to integrate and synthesize the information.

As the energy is synthesized and integrated, it begins to flow back up from the earth and into your body, rising up through your whole body, out your head to fill the bubble that surrounds you. You might find that there are areas in your body where the earth energy is blocked or has restrictions in its flow. If so, while keeping one part of your attention on the flow of energy from the earth, allow the rest of your consciousness to sink down to the place of your subconscious. Be with your subconscious as it experiences this earth energy. You might hold its hand in whatever sense that might be possible. As you do so, you allow your subconscious to have its own experience. Do not get in the way or try to take charge. This allowing makes space for your subconscious to grow, to have better experiences, to feel goodness. As you change your conscious way of being with your subconscious, it naturally heals, learns and grows.

Now allow your natural energy defenses to clear away any pain, dysfunction or unhealthy beliefs or perspectives held in your subconscious from your old way of talking to yourself or past experiences that conflict with your new, kind and gentle approach to your inner consciousness. You may see, feel or experience the positive energies from your natural energy defenses flow all around you, through you and to the space of your subconscious self. Remember, these energies come from true love and goodness, true balance and health and are guided by your inner wisdom. You might want to shift your attention to the flow of love from the earth, coming into your body and flowing to your natural energy defenses. You might want to focus on the images, feelings or knowings coming from your subconscious. You may see, feel or experience the positive shift in vibration of energy within your subconscious or a cleansing of emotions or images. You might also notice that this part of your subconscious holds its own perspectives and beliefs as well as its own free will. Allow yourself to learn how to stop trying to force your will on this part of you and find a place of balance that leads to good health and joy for your whole being. As you simply observe, you might see, feel or experience your natural energy defenses bring this balance to your conscious and subconscious self. Simply allow the energies to flow and the shifts to happen in their own time and in their own way. Hold the expectation that when the time is right, you will feel whole and good and in tune with the flow of positive energy.

Notice that you can hold an expectation without pushing or forcing. It is like placing an order in a restaurant. You expect to receive what you have ordered. In the same way, as you hold this expectation of wholeness, you experience a kind and loving support in your inner being. At the same time, place some of your awareness on the healing that is occurring. You might notice that you are experiencing a kind of faith. Faith in yourself in transforming your connection to your inner self. Faith in your subconscious to be able to change. Faith in your natural energy defenses to bring healing and wholeness. Faith in the love and goodness from the earth energies, and faith in your inner wisdom's solutions that guide and create this positive change. If you or this part of you needs forgiveness in order to experience faith, simply ask that forgiveness flow to and through you. As this forgiveness flows to your whole being, in all of time and all parts of you, notice that this forgiveness carries a strong faith in you, seeing your mistakes, big and small, as a kind of stumble, where you fell down and out of the flow of goodness. This kind of forgiveness is like the kind person who helps you up and dusts you off after you have fallen down. This forgiveness believes that you can stand, and walk and live in the flow of goodness. Allow yourself to feel the forgiveness and feel the faith in yourself. Return your attention to your subconscious. You might notice that it is easier to lightly hold this faith, expectation and gentle intention of wholeness for your subconscious and your whole being.

Now it's time to ground all of these energies into the earth. Make the intention that all of the clearing and healing of beliefs, emotions and energies, all of the expectations and intentions for wholeness, all of the faith, forgiveness and healing flow down your body, out your feet and into the earth. It all flows down, down, down. It goes down to the place where your consciousness connects to the earth. As these energies flow down to this space, the earth energies integrate and synthesize them, allowing you to own them, know them, live them, in stable and grounded ways. The integrated energies flow back up through the earth to you, and you let them in, filling your body and spilling out to fill up the bubble that surrounds you. Take a moment to thank your subconscious. If you like, you can tell it that you will return to spend more time, bring more healing and learn more about it and the goodness it brings to your whole being.

Turn your attention back to your inner wisdom and ask to learn anything else you need to know about the resistance, your connection to your own truth and how to accept your wisdom while experiencing the freedom that is an essential part of your free will and your being. You allow this wisdom to flow to you. It goes to your heart, soul, gut and mind. It flows forward and backward to all time, permeating your present and flowing deeply to parts of your consciousness that are not in the flow of time. It goes deeply into your physical being, into the blueprint of your genetics. You might see it flow to your subconscious, helping your resistance transform and become more empowered. And now, it flows down through the earth to the place where you experience the energies of the earth. You see, feel or experience all of this wisdom synchronize with these earth energies and you experience the energy flow back to you and the bubble that surrounds you.

Now it's time for you to come back to the room and back to your chair, but before you do, let's take a moment to remember all that you have done. You remember learning how to interact with your subconscious with kindness and how your subconscious was able to heal, learn and grow. You remember releasing painful or unbalanced energies and how you were able to give space to your subconscious while lightly holding an expectation and intention of wholeness. You remember the experience of faith in yourself, in your transformation, and in all of the love and goodness for you and for your subconscious. You also remember the light and uplifting energies of forgiveness that believe in you, that help you stand in the flow of goodness and support your own faith in yourself. You remember grounding all of these energies into the earth and allowing them back up to you, your body and the bubble that surrounds you.

Now it's time to return to your room and return to your chair. Allow yourself to feel your body and take a deep breath. Move your fingers and toes. Move your body, and in your own time, open your eyes.

Follow up questions

What did it feel like to be gentle and kind to your subconscious?

If you imagine other areas of your body or your life that are blocked from goodness, is it easy or hard to have kind thoughts and emotions about them? Why?

What part or parts were easy and what parts were hard?

Do you have more work to do with this resistance? If so, what is your commitment to doing that work?

Did this help you feel safer? Please describe.

Exercise 12: Conflict Resolution

Learning how to resolve conflict while feeling safe is a great skill and one we all can improve. You may have your "go-to" reactions to different kinds of conflict. Maybe you get angry. Maybe you want to run away. Maybe you want to get drunk. Maybe you want to grab a weapon. Ask yourself if you are ready to learn new conflict resolution skills and discover other perspectives about conflict in general. Remember, we don't know everything. We only know what we have been taught and what we have decided is true. Also remember that no matter what new "truth" your inner wisdom introduces, you retain your free will. You choose who you want to be and how you want to interact with life, including the parts of your life that present you with conflict.

Grounding Meditation

Do this meditation seated in a chair, with your feet flat on the floor. If you like, you can lay down during the meditation, but if you find yourself falling asleep, you may choose to sit while doing these meditations. Always intend that your meditations be gentle, balanced and healthy for you. Please note that the following meditations include requests or intentions for learning and healing. You do not have to repeat each request or intention in full. Instead, when you read or hear the suggested intention or request, simply say to yourself, "Yes, I intend that."

Take a deep breath and close your eyes. Allow your body to relax. Feel your fingers. Feel your toes. Allow yourself to return to your place in nature. Feel the earth beneath your feet. Smell the air, hear the sounds and feel the temperature. The sun is shining. Feel it on your skin. Sense the softness of the earth under your feet and see the colors of everything around you. Reach out and touch something. Experience its texture. Now expand your awareness to the field of energy that surrounds you. From the inside, or as if you are looking at yourself on a screen, see the bubble of light and energy that surrounds you. You may feel a swirling of energy around you, like a soft, gentle breeze. You might see glowing or swirling colors. Or you might feel a certain pressure, like the perfect weight of covers on a cold winter's night. Now see, feel or experience a cord of energy or a beam of light extend down from the bubble and into the earth. It speeds down into the earth to the place where you connect with pure, clean earth energy, that place of understanding, integration and synchronization of wisdom, energy and being. Intend and allow this beam of light or cord of energy to connect to this place within the earth. You may immediately feel the earth energy flow up the cord or beam and into your bubble, filling it with earth energy. Take a moment to enjoy this flow. Now, come back to full awareness, take a deep breath, and open your eyes.

Imagery Meditation

Now return to your place in nature. You are still inside your bubble, still grounded into the earth and still experiencing the flow of earth energy into your bubble. Now see, feel or experience your connection to your highest inner wisdom. You can feel that flow and energy. You have the connection wherever you are. Take a moment and bask in that flow of positive energy from your highest inner wisdom. It might fill you up. It might fill up your bubble. Just allow yourself to intersect with that energy and with the flow of clean, pure energy from the earth. As you enjoy the flows of these energies, you might notice energetic debris release away from you. It might look or seem like ash floating away, a liquid draining down into the earth or a release of pressure or something else. You might feel like sighing or yawning or twitching. This is normal and a sign that your energy is settling. As you relax more into the flows of these energies, your body might relax more fully.

Now, ask your inner wisdom to teach you what you need to know about conflict and conflict resolution. Imagine that the energy of your inner wisdom is flowing to you. It fills your head, your whole body, your whole mind and your whole heart and gut.

It fills your soul and it extends out the back of your heart to your entire past. It extends out the front of your heart to your entire future and in all directions to the present and deeply into experiences of no time. And it fills all of your genetic material and every part of you. Now, this energy goes down through you and into the earth. It extends down to that place where your bubble is connected to the earth. Allow the inner wisdom energy to flow into that space. And now, allow the earth energy to integrate and synthesize this wisdom. As these energies process, you may have sensations in your body or see images in your mind's eye or have knowings in your gut. This is all fine. As these energies are integrating and synthesizing, you may still feel a strong flow of energy from your head, down through your body and into the earth. This is fine. Just take the time to allow the earth energy to finish its part. Remember, this requires allowing. If you are forcing anything, just take a breath, relax and allow. When the synthesizing is complete, allow that earth energy to flow back up through the earth and into your bubble. If there are blocks to this flow, you can ask your natural energy defenses to remove the blocks. Allow the synthesized earth energy to flow through your feet and legs, through your torso, shoulders, arms, neck, head and out of the top of your head to shower and fill your bubble with this new energy.

Now, ask your inner wisdom to teach your natural energy defenses and teach you how to release any trauma, fear, pain, shame or other uncomfortable emotion or energy relating to conflict or conflict resolution. Again, you see, feel or experience the energy of this wisdom filling up every part of you, from your genetics to your mind, soul, past, present and future. As this energy is flowing, you might feel some of these emotions or energies begin to release from you. When you are ready, allow this wisdom energy to flow down to the earth to be integrated and synthesized. When the integration is finished, allow the earth energy to come up and fill your body and the bubble that surrounds you with that integrated energy.

Now ask your natural energy defenses to protect your memory and imagination space so that you feel the positive energy of your natural energy defenses more strongly than the energies of conflict in the past or future. Ask your natural energy defenses to show you the difference between the energy of your own being and the energy of conflict. Allow yourself to see your being surrounded by love and protection. You see that the conflict energy is outside this positive protection and that your natural energy defenses begin to process and release the conflict energies. You may see, feel or experience your natural energy defenses wrap around you like skin, with the conflict energy somewhere inside your bubble. Remember, your natural energy defenses also live inside your bubble. Those protection energies flow to the conflict and begin to process the conflict. You may want to also ask your inner wisdom to teach you anything else you need to know about this conflict so that you can release it completely. You might notice that as you allow yourself to learn, the conflict energies process more easily. As you allow yourself to learn, you feel less connected to the conflict. As you allow yourself to learn, you feel more empowered and perhaps more at ease about the situation.

If you feel as if you need healing of your energy system or of your being from this conflict, ask your natural energy defenses to heal you so that you can feel more at ease and more comfortable with the past or future. You might see, feel or experience healing energies flowing to some area in your body or in the bubble that surrounds you. As this healing flows, you might also still feel that you are receiving wisdom. Just allow all of these energies to go where they will go and do what they will do while you observe. You might notice that as you receive all of this knowledge, all of the love and protection, all of the healing and changes, the energy of your being shifts. And as the energy of your being shifts, it no longer matches the energy of conflict. Watch as the energy of your entire bubble raises in vibration. As the vibration of your bubble raises, the conflict can no longer sustain itself within your bubble. It completely separates from you and your bubble. Your heart may feel lighter, and your body may feel more relaxed or vibrant. Now, allow all of the wisdom, healing, changes and shifts of energy to move down into the earth where they are integrated, and allow the integrated energies to return to you, filling your body and your bubble.

Now ask your inner wisdom to teach you and your natural energy defenses new conflict resolution techniques that will help you live a more safe and fulfilling life. Ask your natural energy defenses to release old strategies or beliefs that no longer serve you. As before, you allow the wisdom and the healing to fill your whole self, mind, heart, gut, genetics, past, present and future and soul. See, feel or experience the energy flow to all of these spaces. As you do this, the energy around you might feel or seem different, perhaps more expansive or clear or more restful. Now ground this energy into the earth and allow it to integrate and synthesize. As you then allow the integrated energy back up into your body and the bubble that surrounds you, notice how your body feels. Check in with any areas that were healed. Observe or experience the energy there.

Take a moment to relax and enjoy the experience of your new techniques and all that you have learned and experienced. Now, let's take some time to remember all that we have done. You remember accepting wisdom about conflict and its resolution. You remember grounding that energy and the synthesized earth energy filling your body and bubble. You remember releasing energies of past conflict and future worry and how your natural energy defenses surrounded your imagination space with love and protection. You also remember learning new conflict resolution techniques and releasing old ones and how you felt in your body and bubble with this new knowledge and these new techniques.

Now it's time to come back to the room and back to your chair. Imagine your body. Imagine being in your body and being in your room. See and feel yourself seated in your chair. Feel your feet flat on the floor. Move your shoulders around. Move your fingers and toes, and take a deep breath. Slowly, in your own time, open your eyes.

Follow up questions

How easy or difficult was it to connect with the flow of inner wisdom while feeling the energy from the earth flowing to you?

What did you learn about conflict resolution? What new conflict resolution techniques did you see, feel or experience?

What part or parts were easy and what parts were hard?

When you think of conflict that may touch you in the future, how will you act or react differently?

Did this help you feel safer? Please describe.

Exercise 13: You and Your Power

It's time that we cleanse and reclaim our understanding of power. So many people unconsciously react to the idea of power as a force of oppression or domination, corruption or selfishness. At the same time, we know at the deepest levels that humans are powerful beings. We know that our words are powerful, our actions are powerful, our emotions are powerful and that our group efforts can change the world. You are a very powerful being. You cannot escape this. You can block your power. You can give it away. You can hate yourself for it. You nullify it by hoarding your power. But you cannot change your innate nature as a being capable of receiving and giving energies that can create or destroy.

It is my belief that these energies flow through us. They do not come from us. As with energy that can be measured with instruments, vital life force energy always was and always will be. It comes to us and moves through us. We humans have the capacity to change the experience of this energy. We do so through our perceptions, beliefs, attention and intention, but we don't make it. In a sense, we are stewards of power. We are all learning to become better stewards. Some people make mistakes with their power. This leads them into arenas of corruption, violence, hate and resentment. Other people make mistakes with their power by giving or investing it in ways that promote the things they like least. And still, other people make mistakes with their power by rejecting, ignoring or abstaining from positive opportunities due to thinking errors about themselves and the world.

It's time to let go of the notion that any of us is particularly good with power. We are all learning. We are all making mistakes. If we hang ourselves up with notions that only certain people, or only good people or only "fill in the blank" people deserve power, we are lying to ourselves. By engaging in that lie, we block our ability to learn about power. We block the ability to become better stewards and use power in more effective, efficient ways. By denying or misusing power, we ignore opportunities to improve our lives and make the world a better place. The world is calling us to learn new beliefs and techniques around power. It needs us to up our game, improve our lives and spill into the world a cleaner version of power and a new way home to our true nature.

Grounding Meditation

Do this meditation seated in a chair, with your feet flat on the floor. If you like, you can lay down during the meditation, but if you find yourself falling asleep, you may choose to sit while doing these meditations. Always intend that your meditations be gentle, balanced and healthy for you. Please note that the following meditations include requests or intentions for learning and healing. You do not have to repeat each request or intention in full. Instead, when you read or hear the suggested intention or request, simply say to yourself, "Yes, I intend that."

Take a deep breath and close your eyes. Allow your body to relax. Feel your fingers. Feel your toes. Allow yourself to smile. Feel the muscles of your face and the feeling of your skin and your lips and your smile. Now swallow and imagine your consciousness could follow the sensation of swallowing from the inside, as if your awareness could slide from your mouth, down your throat, down through your esophagus and into your stomach. And now your awareness moves backward to a place behind your stomach but in front of your spine. Allow yourself to rest there. Notice if it is easy for your consciousness to reside in this part of your body, or is it difficult or can you go there at all? Is it bright and beautiful or dark and dense? Do you feel mental clarity as your consciousness rests there or are you feeling confusion? Intensify your experience of this space by imagining that you are in there, a small version of you exists within this space between your stomach and spine. What sensations are you experiencing? Is it warm? Cool? Do you feel pleasure or fear? Or is it all just blank? Do you see images or hear sounds? If you like, you can ask this space, "What do I need to know in order for this space to be more balanced, healthy and vital?" Allow yourself to see, feel or experience whatever comes to you. Notice that your attention alone is very healing to this space. Now, make the intention to feel unconditional love and gratitude for this area. You don't have to try to force this emotion. Simply intend unconditional love and gratitude and let them flow through your heart or your being to this space. Just hold the space and energy of unconditional love and gratitude. Now briefly come back to complete awareness of your body, seated in your chair and open your eyes.

Imagery Meditation

Now return to that place behind your stomach and in front of your spine. This area is your power center. Allow yourself to sink into an experience of your personal power in this space. You might see images that relate to your power. You might feel energy or you might have some kind of knowing or insight. Now ask your natural energy defenses to show you the energy of your own power and the energy of your own being within your power center. See your natural energy defenses wrap around the energies of your being and your power, protecting them with love and positive energy. Experience the love and protection in your power center. Imagine that you are inside your power center and the love and protection is streaming to you from all directions. As this energy processes, allow yourself to observe what you naturally visualize, sense or experience.

Now ask your inner wisdom to teach you what you need to know about your power, about your power center and about any dysfunctions there. Let this wisdom into your whole being, your mind, heart and gut. Let it into all time and no time. Let it into your soul and your genetic blueprint. And when you are ready, allow this wisdom to flow down to the earth, synchronize and integrate there and return to you, to your energy center and to the bubble that surrounds you.

Now ask your natural energy defenses to dissolve, resolve and release any past pain or fear or dysfunction you have been holding about your power or holding in your power center. You can also ask your inner wisdom to readjust any beliefs or perspectives you might have about your power or the power used by others. Make it clear that you want beliefs and perspectives that are healthy and balanced, that help you live a safe, empowered and enjoyable life. Watch these changes in your power center, your body and your bubble.

You may see, feel or experience the energy flowing down from the crown of your head, through your body, to your power center and to your natural energy defenses. Notice how you do not have to push, work or use effort for this to happen. You are allowing the flow of wisdom and healing and you are allowing your natural energy defenses to help you while you simply observe and experience. You might also notice the loving earth energy flowing into your system to your natural energy defenses, fueling them with love and vital energy. You might imagine that you are a sponge that can soak up wisdom and healing. You might notice that the wisdom energy looks or seems different than other energies from inside your power center. It might look brighter, more clear. You might notice that there are no heavy strings attached, no agendas or no conditions. You might begin to feel lighter or you might feel as if you are releasing emotion or heavy energies. You may feel as if this space is full, as if there is no room for this inner wisdom energy. If so, ask your natural energy defenses to gently make room for these new energies of wisdom. As these energies integrate and sync together, you may experience insights or knowings that help you understand what is going on with your power. Simply observe and allow. You might also notice that your natural energy defenses are learning and growing, soaking up wisdom, and becoming more empowered, balanced and healthy.

Now allow this wisdom and healing to flow to your whole system, your whole gut, heart, and mind, to your genetics, your soul and all of time and beyond time. Now ground the energy of healing and wisdom into the earth, into that place deep within the earth where you connect to earth energies. Allow the earth energies to integrate and synthesize the healing and wisdom and then let that integrated earth energy flow back up to you, filling your body and your bubble.

Now, ask your natural energy defenses to dissolve, resolve and release any remaining trauma, fear, difficult or unhealthy emotions that interfere with health and balance in your experience of power and your power center. Also ask your natural energy defenses to dissolve, resolve and release any promises or agreements that block your healthy experience of power or any attacks or violations of your power. If you like, ask your higher power to heal any energy leaks, any tears, holes, disintegration or dysfunction and remove any energy parasites in your power center and make it whole. You may see, feel or experience the positive healing energy extend throughout the whole area that lies beneath your ribs and above your belly button. It may seem as if the energy extends out the front and out the back. The energy in this area may become clearer, brighter or more expansive. You may have sensations in other parts of your body. You may receive inner messages or inner knowings. Now ask your higher power and/or inner wisdom to teach you anything else you need to know about how to use your power wisely and safely, with security and joy, maintaining a whole and healthy power center throughout your life.

Again, as you receive this wisdom energy, you may feel as if you are absorbing it, like a sponge, or as a stomach or colon absorbs nutrients. You might even feel as if your natural energy defenses are acting like probiotics, facilitating the process of learning. As you absorb these energies, they go to all of you, your heart, your gut, your mind, your soul. They go to all of time and your whole physical being. You may see your DNA sucking in this energy, or your brain or your heart or your soul. Notice how each becomes brighter and more vital. You might also notice your power center itself begins to change in some way. Just observe. When you are ready, begin to ground all of these energies into the earth. You are grounding all of the wisdom, all of the learning and all of the changes. Those energies flow down through your feet, down from your bubble and into the earth. They go down through the earth to that place where you connect to the earth, where the earth energy helps to integrate and synthesize these energies and call them your own. See, feel or experience this connection to the earth and allow the earth energies to naturally complete the integration. As you observe this natural process, it may feel as if something is being cleaned or organized. Just stay with this experience and allow it to run its course. When you are ready, allow this integrated, synthesized earth energy to flow back up to you, from your feet to your head and out the top of your head to fill up the bubble that surrounds you.

Now it's time for you to come back to the room and back to your chair, but before you do, let's take a moment to remember all that you have done. You remember discovering your power center in the space behind your stomach and in front of your spine. You remember seeing this space, giving love and acceptance to it and from the perspective of this space, learning from your inner wisdom and raising the vibration of your beliefs. You remember how your natural energy defenses removed blocks and old emotions and pains and how the wisdom found its way to your power center and to you. You remember soaking it in like a sponge and how you learned to be safe, secure and fulfilled in your experiences of power. You remember what it felt like to ground, integrate and synthesize these energies of wisdom in partnership with the earth, and you remember receiving and being filled with the integrated energies in your body and the bubble that surrounds you.

Now it's time to return to your room and return to your chair. Allow yourself to feel your body and take a deep breath. Move your fingers and toes. Move your body, and in your own time, open your eyes.

Follow up questions

Describe what your power center looked like and how it felt.

What insights, if any, did you receive about your power?

What part or parts were easy and what parts were hard?

Do you feel safe with your power? Why?

Did this help you feel safer? Please describe.

Exercise 14: Addiction

When I asked my inner wisdom, "What do I need to know about addiction?" the answer I got was, "It's a holding pattern." Along with this message came the image of a plane waiting to land, and also a bunch of people at a gate at the airport, waiting to board that plane. Interesting. Then it occurred to me that I was plugging into my own personal wisdom about myself. Then I asked my inner wisdom, "What does the public need to know about addiction?" I immediately felt a huge wave of fear and heavy weight along with an image of a person trying to shove dark heaviness away from themselves. What I took from this is that our fear and judgement around addiction is getting in the way of doing something productive with it. Let's face it. We are all addicted to things in life. I'm addicted to coffee, certain foods, audiobooks and probably Facebook. I should probably drink less and take more adventures and risks. I know that I have a lot of room to grow. I bet that is true for each and every one of us. In that regard, I think that this meditation exercise is potentially useful for all of us.

On the other hand, I know that certain types of addictions are torture. As a lawyer, I saw what addiction did to my clients and what it did to their families. I'm not going to try to put a pretty pink bow on this issue or try to minimize it in any way. Instead, I offer the following exercise as one way to get in touch with your inner wisdom about your addictions and learn how to use your natural energy defenses to support you into your next version of empowerment. My greatest hope is that you can transform your torture or holding pattern or any other impact of addiction into growth and fulfillment.

Grounding Meditation

Do this meditation seated in a chair, with your feet flat on the floor. If you like, you can lay down during the meditation, but if you find yourself falling asleep, you may choose to sit while doing these meditations. Always intend that your meditations be gentle, balanced and healthy for you. Please note that the following meditations include requests or intentions for learning and healing. You do not have to repeat each request or intention in full. Instead, when you read or hear the suggested intention or request, simply say to yourself, "Yes, I intend that."

Take a deep breath and close your eyes. You are back in your beautiful place in nature. Take a moment to really see, feel and experience this place. It is the perfect season. Your vision is crisp and clear. You can hear the lovely and tranquil sounds of this place, and the smells are like a gentle perfume. Feel how safe it is to simply enjoy this place. Perhaps you feel your natural energy defenses cradling or protecting you. Perhaps the earth itself feels soft or friendly. Notice how this beautiful place in nature cushions you from any cares or discomforts. It is a place where you can be and be yourself in tranquility and goodness. Allow your natural energy defenses to take care of anything that is less than tranquil and good. For this moment, enjoy. Now it's time to come back to the room. Take a deep breath, come back to your body, feel your body and in your own time open your eyes and take another deep breath.

Imagery Meditation

Close your eyes. Return to your beautiful place in nature, and return to the tranquility. Take a look around until you see a path. Go to the path and begin to follow it. You might feel the surface of the path beneath your feet. It may be dirt or grass or even pavement or some other surface. As you walk along, feel the surface of the path and see what is near you. You might want to reach out and touch something near you and feel its texture and feel the gentle warmth of the sun. In the distance, you now see a large stand of trees, a forest. As you near this forest, you see that your path leads into the forest and under the trees. Go ahead and follow the path into the forest. Feel how it is a little cooler here. You see the sunlight filtering down through the leaves and branches and your eyes adjust to the light. Smell the loamy scent of the trees and the earth. See the woodland flowers and mushrooms and plants. Perhaps there are animals or birds or other creatures that make up this vibrant landscape. As you continue along the path, it gently curves, and as you round the curve, you see a clearing. You see the sun shining down here, with the tall trees standing in a ring around this precious spot. As you stand at the threshold of this clearing, you notice that your natural energy defenses surround this clearing, bringing protection and keeping out anything that does not serve your highest good. As you step into the sunlight of the clearing, you gaze up, into the blue of the sky and allow the sunlight to fall upon your skin. You notice that the sunlight feels different, more gentle, more magical and more vital. Take a moment to drink in the vitality of this sunlight while your natural energy defenses surround and protect you.

Now turn your attention to the center of this clearing where you see a kind of disturbance in the earth. As you focus on the earth in the center of the clearing, you begin to understand that it is or represents the wounds, misconceptions or fears that you carry. It may look as if the earth in this place is wounded or scarred or you might see a shape or something else that represents your wounds. Notice that from where you stand, it is safe to simply see these wounds and allow the sunlight to fall here. To be. Feel the safety flowing from your natural energy defenses. Really experience how those defenses are fueled by love from the earth. Perhaps you experience the love flowing up from the earth and into your body. Notice how you can feel goodness and/or love and/or vitality flowing to you even with the wounds in the center of the clearing. You might also notice that the forest itself is supporting you. All of the trees and the plants, all of the insects and creatures and even the molecules of air are holding space, helping you to allow your wounds, misconceptions and fears to heal and realign and also helping you learn and grow through the process. This place is so friendly to you, and this friendliness feels good.

Now ask the sunlight to help you understand what you need to know about your wounds, fears and misconceptions and also about your life or yourself so that you can heal and become free from those things that have chained you to addiction. Allow the sunlight to fall upon you. Soak in this information. Feel as if it is giving you keys of understanding, new perspectives and perhaps higher beliefs. You may see energetic keys flowing into your system, unlocking new knowledge. You may experience this new knowledge flowing into you and flushing out the old. Ask the sunlight to help you see, feel and know how to live in safety, security and happiness without your wounds and without your addictions. As the sunlight flows to you, allow your perspectives to change. Focus on allowing the gentle sunlight into your eyes. Into your nose and sinuses. And into your mouth and tongue. Now allow the sunlight into your skin. Know that this is changing your perspectives and your beliefs and your understandings about safety, security, happiness and wholeness. Notice that as you change, the area at the center of the clearing is also changing.

Now focus again on the friendliness of the forest around you and the protection that your natural energy defenses bring to you. Now ask the sunlight to bring you relief from the pain of your wounds, fears and old unhealthy beliefs and to perhaps teach you how to receive or absorb this relief and let it in. Notice how this sunlight circulates through your whole self, your mind and gut, your heart and soul, filling up you and all of time, filling up any spaces within you that seem separate from time and easily flushing out wounds that belong to other people, places or events and raising the vibration of your beliefs so that you can easily release that which does not belong to you and that which no longer matches you.

Now notice that the forest surrounding you begins to sound with a gentle churring or whirring noise. As this sound increases in volume, everything begins to vibrate with its patterns. You, the trees, the earth, the air and your wounds and fears are all vibrating to the sound of the forest. It is raising the vibration of all things, all of your experiences, all of your thoughts, all of your emotions, and all of the things that you have been carrying. You notice as this vibration persists, the wounds, emotions and beliefs in the center of the clearing begin to break apart and float away or simply disintegrate. As they change and transform in sync with the vibration of the forest, ask the sunlight to teach you how to live and thrive without the old things and without the addictions. Ask the sunlight how to attract and thrive with new energies and new experiences.

Again, you allow the sunlight to flow through your whole self, your whole physical, emotional and spiritual being, through all of time and beyond. Now allow all that you have learned, all of the changes and transformations and healings to flow down through your body and into the earth. It all goes down, down, down to that place where you connect to the earth. Allow these energies to integrate and synthesize with the earth energies. Now allow the synthesized and integrated energies to come back up through the earth to you, filling up your body and filling up the bubble that surrounds you. You may also see that some of that energy has come up into the clearing, filling up the whole space and perhaps completing the healing of the wounds within the clearing. If any wounds or painful thoughts or emotions remain, know that it's okay. You have plenty of time to come back to this friendly, safe place with its magical sunlight and bring more goodness, healing and wisdom to your being and help you become more in touch with your ability to live in freedom, happiness, safety and security.

It's time now to come back to your room and back to your chair, but before you do, let's remember all that you have done. You remember your place in nature and its tranquility. You remember the path, the forest and the clearing with its wounds in the center. You remember the magical sunlight, the natural energy defenses surrounding the clearing and the friendliness and support of the forest. You remember learning about your wounds and addictions and how to live without them. You remember the keys of understanding coming to you, and the changes in perspectives in all of your senses. You remember releasing pain and how the natural sounds of the forest intensified to help you release pain and raise your vibration. You remember grounding all of this learning, transformation and healing down into the earth where it was integrated and synthesized, and you remember allowing the integrated energy back up into your body and your bubble to live and enjoy it.

Now it's time to come back to the room and back to your chair. So say goodbye to the clearing, knowing that you can come back any time to learn more. Return back through the forest, following the path. Go back to your special place in nature, and when you are ready, come back to your body in your chair, in your room, in your current time. Feel yourself seated in your chair with your feet flat on the floor. Move your shoulders around and take a deep breath in and out. Slowly, in your own time, open your eyes.

Note: You may have to do this meditation several times in order to feel that you are complete with it. Try in each meditation to move around the clearing to a different perspective. Often we must see obstacles or challenges from all perspectives in order to be able to move past them. It is my belief that the wounds or challenges of today are the teachers that prepare us for what we need to know and be able to do in the future. And I believe that when we have learned from the wounds and challenges, we can move past them into a different and more whole way of being.

Follow up questions

Do you, or did you have addictions? If so, what are they? What will you do differently in relation to these addictions?

What did you see or experience in the clearing? Did it seem different at the end of the meditation?

What part or parts were easy and what parts were hard?

Do you feel different after doing this meditation? If so, how?

Did this help you feel safer? Please describe.

Bonus Section

After doing the above meditation myself, I found that it was pretty easy to give up my glass (or two) of wine every night. To my dismay, I found that my attraction for the wine was covering an even deeper unhealthy attraction to sugar. The sugar addiction was a beast! I was going out of my gourd trying to fight it. Finally it occurred to me that there was more for me to learn about my inner unhealthy attractions. It truly felt as if the sugar was pulling my attention, my emotions and my energies to it, just like a magnet. So, I provide the following addition to the above meditation. Please note that if you are working on an addiction to life's basics like food, sex, money, exercise, etc., you will need to alter the attraction, not end it. Make sure you are asking to learn, following your inner wisdom and aiming for health and balance.

Also note that this exercise can apply to addictions or sticky attractions to people, places, things and emotional states or experiences, such as violence, hatred or oppression. Please do not mistake this as some kind of meanness or blaming. If a person has unconscious attractions to something they experienced in the past, they do. It's better to confront it in a neutral way, learn about it, resolve it and move on. Remember, it's all just energy, it is not a statement of a person's worth or competence or intelligence. It's just energy. And remember that there is a difference between the energy of your being and the energies that are coming into your experience. You are great, just as you are, and you are not the thoughts, emotions or energies that flow through you. If you want to learn more and shift your energy, try out the following.

Bonus Meditation

Find a place where you can sit down with your feet flat on the floor and in a time that is reserved only for you. Close your eyes and take a nice deep breath. Return to your place in nature. Take a moment to feel its tranquility and then follow the path to the forest, to the clearing and to that place where you have healed and resolved wounds, fears and limitations that have caused your addictions. Walk out to the center of the clearing, feel the sunlight on your face and on your body. Check in with your connection to the earth. See, feel or experience the loving, healthy flow of earth energy up into your body and your bubble. You might feel the positive energy from the sunlight flowing in through your head, filling your body. Notice that as you relax, the flows up and down through your body gently increase.

Now ask your inner wisdom to teach you what you need to know about the unhealthy attraction and the magnetic or attractive quality of your addiction. If you like, you can also ask to learn what is a better option. You can ask something like this, "Inner wisdom, teach me what I need to know about my addiction and attraction to sugar and how I can change and/or adopt something better. Adjust my beliefs and perceptions to foster healthy and balanced attractions." Imagine that this wisdom is coming to you through the sunlight. It flows down through your head, filling your brain and your mind, it flows down through your torso, filling your heart and overflowing out the back to the past, out the front to your future, in all directions to present time and to no time and deep into your heart to your soul. It goes to your belly and deep into the sensations and rhythm and pulse of your body, including your whole nervous system and your genetic material. It goes down through your legs and feet into the earth, down to the place where you connect to earth energies. You allow the wisdom to integrate with the earth energies there. Now allow the integrated energies back up to you and to the bubble that surrounds you.

Now ask your inner wisdom or higher power to make the changes necessary so that you are no longer attracted to the subject of your addiction and that it is no longer attracted to you. Ask that these changes leave you attracted and attractive to that which is healthy, balanced and in alignment with your highest purpose. If you like, you can ask for help with any deeper or underlying issues so that your whole being can experience health and balance. Again, you see the healing energy flow down to you, filling your head and mind, your heart and gut, filling all time, no time, your soul and genetic material. You might also see, feel and experience these energies permeate the bubble that surrounds you. Allow those energies to flow down to your connection with the earth and let the earth energies synchronize and integrate them. Now it's time to allow those energies to return to you and the bubble that surrounds you.

Ask your inner wisdom and natural energy defenses to help you resolve any pains, emotions or thoughts about your now former addiction and your old ways of being. You may see, feel or experience this healing by goodness and wisdom flowing to the wounds represented in the clearing. Allow your inner wisdom to teach you the difference between your being and its energies and the energies related to those wounds. Allow your inner wisdom to teach you how to process and release the energies related to those wounds so that you know how to cope with the challenges they represent. Now ask your inner wisdom to teach you how to give self-love to the part of you that held those wounds, how to forgive the unforgivable and to love the unlovable and to fill the appetite that you had for your addiction with self-love, self-forgiveness, self-compassion and self-acceptance. And ask your inner wisdom to teach the part of you that is hungry for love, life, or whatever drove your addiction, how to accept that goodness, process that energy and claim it for your own. Also ask your inner wisdom to teach you how to accept and experience the protection of your natural energy defenses at these deeper levels. Again, you see, feel or experience all of this wisdom flow to you, filling you and the bubble that surrounds you. Let it into your whole mind, your whole heart and soul, all of time and no time and your whole gut, body and genetic material.

Now take a moment to imagine what you want to replace your addiction. Perhaps you want new friends who are dear to you or maybe you want the resources and time to travel or have adventures, or you might want to explore other avenues that bring you joy and pleasure. Even if you don't know how you could possibly get what it is that your heart wants, put your attention on it. Allow your heart to feel love for it. Now ask your inner wisdom to adjust your beliefs and perceptions and the magnetics in your system so that you are attracted to this new good and that it is attracted to you. Allow all of these changes to flow through your entire mind, heart, soul, time, no time, body and genetic material. Now let all the healing, all the self-love, all of the learning and all of the changes flow down to the place where you connect to the earth. Allow the earth energies to mix and mingle with this healing and wisdom. They synchronize and integrate. And now, the integrated and synthesized energies flow back up to you and to the bubble that surrounds you.

And now it's time to return to the room and return to your chair, but before you do, let's remember all we have done. You remember your place in nature and its tranquility, you remember the clearing in the forest. You remember learning about the attractive quality of your addiction and changing the attraction so that you are no longer attracted to it and it is no longer attracted to you. You remember healing deeper wounds and how to give and receive self-love, self-forgiveness and self-acceptance. You remember learning how to replace your addiction with what you want and how to be attracted to and attractive to that new good. You remember what it felt like to ground all of these energies into the earth, claiming them for yourself and letting them return to you, filling your body, your bubble and your whole being with these upgraded and safe energies.

Now come back to your room and back to your chair. Come back to your body. Feel yourself in your body. Feel how good it feels to be in your body with all of these new energies flowing through you. Move your body. Move your toes. Move your fingers. Shrug your shoulders. Now take a deep breath and open your eyes.

Follow up questions

What did you learn about the attractive quality of your former addiction? Did that teach you anything more about life in general?

What did you learn about self-love, self-forgiveness or self-acceptance?

What part or parts were easy and what parts were hard?

What did you learn about what you want instead of your old addiction? Is there anything you can do to enhance the feeling attraction to it and accept the experience of being attractive to it without having to earn, work or become more deserving in some way?

Did this help you feel safer? Please describe.

Personal Note: This issue of addiction has been a huge area of growth for me. I felt very stretched in doing both of these meditations regarding addiction. I offer this insight into my personal experience, not as an indulgence in navel gazing, but as an example of how you might work with yourself when addressing deep issues. When I did the above meditation, I found that under the sugar addiction was a tendency to connect with other people in a way to band together to fight, complain about, struggle against or dislike different experiences of lack. It was an, "Ain't it awful" habit that gave me a feeling of connection. That feeling of connection, security and energy (albeit, sort of yucky energy) was a fuel to this part of my being. I became aware that I was being driven in that direction by my own sense of inner lack and that until I could resolve that, I could change the circumstances of my connections, but they would always somehow contain that energy of lack because that was how my being was using energy.

Once I realized this, I asked my inner wisdom to teach me what I needed to know about it. I got nothing, no message, no direction, no picture in my mind's eye. So, I just sat with it in the attitude of, "I'm waiting...." Then, love, for this lack filled, hungry part of myself began to blossom in my belly. I began to realize and feel that I love this part of myself. Even if a part of myself is needy, as mortifying as that is, it's okay. I can and do love this part of myself. It doesn't have to be beautiful. Even if it's not great at everything, that's okay. I can still love it. It's just an area that has stuff to learn and has room for growth. I can live and exist even if this hunger or neediness never changes. It's just okay. Once I confronted the neediness and knew I was okay regardless, it was much easier to see what was driving it. In my case, there were a few layers of the typical stuff like fear and abandonment and simply not knowing how to cope. Once I could see it, I could work with it. I could learn how to process and release those energies, see that they are quite different from the energy of my being and that knowing how to confront and release those energies makes life a lot easier.

This is how energy healing works. You find a way to connect with the stuff that really annoys or drives you, you learn how to stop running away from it or stop pushing it away, and then you learn how to process and release it and replace it with something better. As your inner being experiences all of these shifts, your thinking and your experiences shift for the better. This is what empowerment is, and this is why it is worth the time and the effort to do meditations like this or any other activity that brings you empowerment.

Exercise 15: Your Place in the Flow, When Others Are Not

I originally titled this section, "Narcissism and Other Personality Disorders." I was drawn in that direction, not because I am an expert in such matters, but because I think we have all confronted people who have strong techniques to unground us, interfere with our flow of goodness and drag us into their perspective of lack and woe or conflict. I used to fight with those kinds of people or at least adopt an attitude of judgement for them. Now, I see them as people who strengthen our abilities to stay grounded, strengthen our flow of goodness, deepen our commitment to the good and focus us more deeply on that which is effective in making the world a better place. I am not going to lie, this is a challenge. To describe this challenge, I need to describe the energy involved.

I first want to talk about the person who uses techniques to disconnect us from our flow of life force energy in ways that take our energy. I call this person the Obstructor. First of all, the Obstructor is not connected to flows of vital life force energy from their own natural source energy. They cannot renew themselves, and they need vital energy to survive. To them, every person is a potential source of sustenance. If you think I am describing a predator, I am. But understand that to them, this is life or death. I believe that it is literal. They must have energy to live. If they are blocked from source, they must find it through other ways. If you are their prey, it is not personal, and it really has nothing to do with you, except as a vehicle for their survival. At the same time, each time this person steals, manipulates or otherwise takes another person's energy, it is a violation of that person. Not only does the Obstructor feel the shame of that violation, he or she must deal with the negative energy coming from the person who was violated. This further occludes their own personal connection to source energy and digs them deeper into their hole.

Before you think that we should save, fix or uplift these people, I advise you to think again. People change and grow when they are ready. It takes true strength for an Obstructor to face their own shame and unclutter their inner space. They will not do it on a timeline that suits you or anyone else. By all means, pray for them, learn how to hold compassion for them, but do not get hooked into their struggle for energy. Their gift to you is to give you the clarity and incentive to learn how to give love to yourself and how to team up with your inner ability to allow love to protect you. This work requires you to learn more about self-love, discernment and your authority within your own sphere of energy.

To me, Obstructors are like geodes, coarse and unappealing on the outside, with the good stuff trapped within. It is only when life cracks them open can they reveal the good within. The best thing you can do for an Obstructor is to turn your attention to yourself. Find the places within you that need to be opened up to positive energy and learn how to do so with grace and ease. Do this for your own good, but also know that as you prove that it can be done, others will instinctively know the change within you, and if it is right for them, they will be inspired to find their own path to their source energy.

I also want to talk about a different kind of person. I'll call this person the Depressor. I am not talking about a person who is depressed. Instead, this is the "Debbie Downer" person. Their glass is always half empty. The world is a veil of tears, and nothing you say or do can inspire joy or even contentment. This person is not taking your energy, they are inviting you to depress your energy, to slow it down to their frequency. They can't exist in an atmosphere of security or happiness or goodness, so they are inviting you to step into their energy environment so the two of you can connect. In their world of woe, they are lonely. We all yearn for connection. Their desire to connect is natural and your desire to connect with them is natural as well. Yet, it is like going to a friend's house for a playdate and their house is a mess. You can't find anything, everything is dirty and it's just a bummer. You try to invite them to your place, but they just can't make it there.

You might think, why do they live like that? I think it's all unconscious. We all carry a myriad number of beliefs that we are given through our upbringing, our society, the books we read, the advertisements we watch, the communities we live in and more. At the same time, I think it is very easy to experience disappointment, lack or other sadness and unconsciously adopt beliefs such as, "This is what I deserve" or "That is how things are" or "I'm safer if I expect the worst" or simply, "I suck." For this person, connection to source energy is available, but clouded or conditioned by these disempowering beliefs. Again, this person will change when they are ready to change. Until they are ready to let go of their grip on their depressed world and reach for something better, it will feel safer to live as they are. I think it is more an issue of faith in themselves and faith in life than an issue of courage. I have so much compassion for these people and so much hope.

At the same time, I know that I am not willing to step into their world. If I do, I become ungrounded and unhappy. To me, it is a commitment to myself to stay in the light, the flow of positive life force energy and hold a different energy from the Depressors in the world. It is my hope that by doing so, I give them incentive to do what is necessary to up their energy and step into their own flow of goodness. To be fair, I must admit that I am not perfect in this. I meditate or do energy work on myself every day to stay in the flow. Sometimes, I get ungrounded. Just like everyone else, I have to recommit to myself, and reconnect. It is my hope that the following exercise will help you gain your own perspectives on how to stay in the flow of goodness when others are not.

Grounding Meditation

Do this meditation seated in a chair, with your feet flat on the floor. If you like, you can lay down during the meditation, but if you find yourself falling asleep, you may choose to sit while doing these meditations. Always intend that your meditations be gentle, balanced and healthy for you. Please note that the following meditations include requests or intentions for learning and healing. You do not have to repeat each request or intention in full. Instead, when you read or hear the suggested intention or request, simply say to yourself, "Yes, I intend that."

Take a deep breath and close your eyes. Take a moment and remember our first exercise with its beautiful place in nature, the walk and the house or castle with its spire. Go back to that place. Feel the nature all around you. Enjoy the beautiful day. Feel the earth beneath your feet. Feel your connection to the earth there. Now, go back to the castle or house with its spire. Find your way there, find your way to the front door. Place your hand on the plaque next to the door and watch the door open to you. You see the stairs before you and you easily glide up them. When you reach the landing, you pass by the room with all of its curious machinery and find another room filled with trunks and wardrobes and storage cabinets. You are immediately attracted to three beautiful boxes. One is long and slim. The next is square, and the third is small and deep. You first open the square box and find a lovely crown within. It is made of precious metal and precious gems. You somehow know that it will fit you perfectly and that it is for you to take, use and own. You next open the long box. In it is a scepter or staff, a thin but strong rod of wood with a gem set in gold affixed to the top. This too, you know, is yours and is important for you. The final box contains a pendant on a chain. This also carries a sense of familiarity, as if you somehow misplaced it and are delighted to find it again. You take these three lovely treasures up to the top of the spire and hold them above your head. Ask the crystal, the conveyer of your inner wisdom, to flood these treasures with the knowledge and energies necessary to help you stand in your own light and live in your own energy environment of good. You might see, feel or experience the crystal energies flow to the treasures. They might buzz or vibrate in your hands or become brighter. When the flow dwindles, come back to your body and the room, open your eyes and take a deep breath.

Imagery Meditation

Close your eyes. Take a moment to focus on your breathing. And now return to the castle and return to the top of the spire, standing beneath the crystal, holding your three treasures. Go ahead and slip the pendant over your head. Notice that the pendant rests right over your energetic heart space, where love flows. If it is too heavy or the wrong size, ask the crystal to make it light, easy and the exact right size and weight. Ask the crystal to teach you how to live with it being perfect for you. Let the energy of this information fill you up.

Now don the crown. It rests easily and lightly at the top of your head. It fits your head perfectly. If it is too big or too small, ask the crystal to shrink or expand it and to teach you how to live with it being exactly right for you. Again, the energy of learning fills you up.

Now pick up the scepter. Its top should be level with, or right above the crown of your head, and it should be comfortable to hold and light to carry. If it is the wrong size, again, ask the crystal to change it to the right size and teach you how to thrive, using and enjoying it. As you allow this learning energy to flow through you, notice how you feel with the pendant, crown and staff.

When you feel ready, ask your inner wisdom to teach you anything else you need to know in order to use these three treasures and integrate them into your life. If you like, you can ask your inner wisdom to readjust your beliefs and perspectives so that you can feel safe with and trust your authority, discernment and self-love and that you are allowed to experience and enjoy these energies. See, feel or experience that wisdom energy come down into your head and down into your body, into your gut, your heart, your soul and your mind. It goes backward and forward through time and to the present. It goes into any places in your consciousness that do not experience time. It goes to your whole body and all of its genetics. And now, it goes down into the earth, down to that place where you experience your connection to the earth and your understanding of yourself in your life and in the universe. Let the wisdom energy synthesize and integrate in this space. And when you are ready, allow this synthesized energy to come back up to you, into your body, through your body, flowing out the top of your head and filling up your bubble.

Now remember that you are at the top of the spire, beneath the beautiful crystal. Take the scepter or staff in your hand and tap it on the floor three times to activate the flow of your own personal authority. As this energy begins to flow to and through you, you might notice that your body fills with your authority and your bubble also fills with this energy. It comes up through the earth and into your body as if it was waiting there, ready for you to call it in. Also notice the authority energy coming into your being through your head. You might see, feel or experience a light or pulsing in the center of your head, as if you have an organ there that takes in authority energy from the crystal, processes it and sends it out in all directions. Notice also that the gem at the top of the scepter is also lit with the energy of your authority, and it too is sending energy in all directions. Some of that authority energy also moves down into your body to circulate through your system.

Intend to see, feel or experience how this authority energy is uniquely your own and how it is protected by your natural energy defenses. Notice that the more you relax and allow this energy to flow into you and your space, the easier and more efficiently it flows. Now ask the crystal to dissolve, resolve and release beliefs or ways of being that block your authority. Ask the crystal to replace those beliefs with what is right for you and what will make it easy for you to allow the authority energy to say no to the things you don't want and yes to the things you do want. Allow the crystal to teach you that the energy of your authority is more real than the energy of what you do not want.

You allow all of the energy of the learning and changes to flow to your whole mind, your whole heart, your whole gut and your whole physical being. It fills your soul. It goes out the back and front of your heart to all of time, including the present, and it goes to those spaces or places between time. You now easily ground these learning energies into the earth, to that place where you connect with beautiful earth energies. Allow all of this learning to integrate and synthesize and when that is done, allow the renewed, synthesized energies to flow back to you, filling both you and the bubble that surrounds you.

Focus again on the flow of authority energy coming into your head and in through your feet. Notice how your authority energy is not a wall or a shield. It is not a weapon or a judgement or a gift or even a healing. Instead, as you become one with this flow of your authority, you may realize that your authority is simply a part of you, a part of your being and the energy that flows to and through you is flowing because of this vital part of you. As you relax or sink deeper into the flow of this energy, you may experience your staff or scepter begin to buzz or vibrate with the energy of authority within your sphere. If you like, you can ask your natural energy defenses to dissolve, resolve and release any pain or fear you have from past experiences of authority. As you allow this healing, see, feel or experience the soothing, revitalizing energies to flow to the spaces that need support.

Now it's time to switch your attention to your crown and discernment. Ask your inner wisdom to teach you and your natural energy defenses what you need to know about discernment and how to use it. Allow that learning to flow through your whole being and your natural energy defenses, ground that energy and let it return to you. Now, use your authority energy to speak out into your bubble, "I intend to experience my highest discernment." Watch that energy flow out of your throat, in front and back, to your bubble. Let it transform and move as it will, and let it interact with you. Now watch as discernment comes up from your connection to the earth and down from the crystal. It fills your body, mind and being and it fills the space around you. You become the energy of discernment. Every particle of your being vibrates to the frequency of discernment. All the space around you is filled with discernment. If you like, you can ask your natural energy defenses to remove old energies or memories of lack of discernment or even negative beliefs or perspectives you still hold from past lack of discernment. As your natural energy defenses dissolve, resolve and release old energies, you may experience your crown also resonating with these clear and positive discerning energies. You may also experience a holistic kind of discernment, going to thoughts, emotions, sensations and knowings. See how your natural energy defenses protect your discernment.

Now switch your attention to your pendant and self-love. Using your authority energy, intend to experience self-love and with your discernment energy, intend to see or experience self-love. You might see, feel or experience your authority energy flow out of your throat, to your bubble. You might see, feel or experience the discernment flow through your body and out your forehead to your bubble. You feel the staff vibrate with the energy of authority. You use this authority to choose self-love. And you feel the crown vibrate with the energy of discernment that allows you to know self-love, feel it and experience it fully. And now, you see, feel or experience your pendant vibrate with the energy of self-love. It flows from the pendant, into your heart. You might feel your heart drinking it in. You might experience it flowing out the back of your heart to your whole past. It might fill your heart, sending out rippling waves to your whole present. And it might flow out the front of your heart to your whole future. It flows out to the bubble that surrounds you so that you and the energy that surrounds you are self-love. And if this is difficult for you, ask your natural energy defenses and/or your higher power to give you the healing necessary and change your beliefs so that you can receive and experience self-love in your whole space and your whole being. See, feel, experience and allow this healing flowing through your whole being and all of time and see that along with this healing comes protection of your self- love by your natural energy defenses.

Now, if you like, you can pick a gesture, like a smile or pressing two fingers together. Do this gesture, intending to anchor these sensations into your being with this gesture, so now when you do this gesture in the future, you will immediately be in touch with your authority, discernment and self-love. Now allow all the learning, all the changes, all the healing flow through your whole being, your body and all of your genetic material. Let it fill your mind, gut and heart. Allow it to flow out the back of your heart to the past, out the front of your heart to the future and out all directions to the present. Allow it to flow to non-time and allow it to fill your soul. Now see, feel and experience this energy flow down through your body, out your feet and down through the earth. Let it go to that place where you connect to earth energies and allow the earth to integrate and synthesize them. Now allow the integrated energies back up to you, into your feet, throughout your body and out the top of your head to the bubble that surrounds you.

Take a moment to feel gratitude for these energies, for the learning and for the healing. You now remember all that you have done, the place in nature, the house or castle, and the beautiful crystal at the top of the spire. You remember the staff, crown and pendant and how you were able to use them to fill up with the energies of authority, discernment and self-love. You remember how the authority flowed through your head and throat and through the gem in the scepter. You remember how the crown easily magnetized discernment to and through you, allowing you to see more clearly. You remember how the pendant drew self-love to your heart, filling it and helping self-love flow to areas in your life that need more love. You remember the gesture that anchored the experiences of authority, discernment and self-love into your body so that when in the future you initiate the gesture, you will be in the flow of these important, joyful energies.

Now it's time to come back to the room and back to your chair. You can leave the crystal room, going down through the other rooms, down the staircase, out of the building, along the path, back to your place in nature.

And now come back to your room, back to your chair, back to your body and back to your current time and place. Feel your feet flat on the floor. Move your shoulders around and take a deep breath in and out. Slowly, in your own time, open your eyes.

Note: When focusing on self-love in the above exercise, you may be drawn to focus on giving yourself other loving experiences such as self-forgiveness, self-acceptance, self-compassion or self-approval. I see these as subsets of self-love. My metaphor for this is when white light goes through a prism, we see all the colors of the rainbow. These colors together make up white light. I believe all the aspects of self-love come together to make the whole of what we experience as self-love. In this way, you may want to play with using the above meditation to bring different aspects of self-love into your experience by focusing on filling your heart with self-forgiveness or another aspect of self-love during the meditation.

Follow up questions

Do you feel more able to stay grounded in the flow of goodness, even if the people around you are detached from their own source energy? If so, describe what you will do when you next meet people who are inviting you to detach from your flow.

Did you learn anything about yourself from this meditation? If so, what?

What did your crown, pendant and scepter or staff look like?

How do you feel about having authority, discernment and self-love?

Do you believe you have the right to be happy and fulfilled when other people are not? If so, why? If not, why?

Did this help you feel safer? Please describe.

Bonus Section

In this section, we will try out your new tools of authority, discernment and self-love. Sometimes it takes practice to get the feel of a new approach to energy.

Bonus Meditation

Find a comfortable place to sit down. Close your eyes with your feet flat on the floor. Take a deep breath and turn your attention to the previous meditation. Return to your place in nature. See the sights, smell the scents and feel all of the sensations of that place. When you are ready, return to the castle with its spire. Return to the top of the spire, and notice that you still have the scepter or staff, the crown and the pendant. Make sure that you are wearing the crown and the pendant and holding the staff. Feel the smooth texture of the staff. Notice the gems set into the ornament at the top of the scepter. See the color and possibly the sun glittering off the facets of the gem or gems. Notice that you have a bubble of energy that surrounds you and your natural energy defenses are protecting you.

Now think of something that you clearly want to say no to. Use the scepter to tap the floor three times to initiate the flow of your authority energy. See yourself and your bubble filling up with your authority energy. You might experience the authority energy as a specific color or texture or sensation. Think of what you want to deny or exclude and say “No.” Allow the authority energy to easily flow out of your head in all directions and out of your throat, as if it goes out your throat as you say “No.” your bubble is filled with your authority and the gem at the top of the scepter shines and pulses with light and energy. This operates without any force of will or emotion. As you allow the authority energy to work within your bubble, you might see the energy transform in some way or see it empowering your bubble. You might see, feel or experience the transformed energy moving back into your body and interacting with your body in some way, perhaps creating changes or adding energies. All of this happens within your bubble, your powerful space of flow and energy.

Now think of something you clearly want to say yes to. See yourself holding your staff, your personal authority energy is flowing and has filled you and your bubble. Say, "Yes." See, feel or experience the authority energy flow through your head in all directions and out of the scepter and also out your throat, moving into your bubble. As the authority energy continues to flow out of your head and throat, watch the energy. See, feel or experience how it transforms or takes on a life of its own. Experience what it does or how it works within your bubble or to your bubble and within your body. Allow the authority energy to have complete autonomy. Notice how good it feels to simply allow your authority energy to flow out and perhaps how empowering it feels to allow the energy to change your bubble and your body. You may also see, feel or experience your natural energy defenses combining or working with the authority energies.

Now it's time to try out the energy of discernment. Remember your crown and intend the energy of discernment to fill up your body and your bubble. You might see, feel or experience the crown, acting as a sort of magnet, drawing discernment into your head and in through your feet. Ask your inner wisdom and the discernment energy to show you the difference between the energy of your own being and the energies of other people and their emotions, thoughts and intentions. You may see, feel or experience positive energy flowing in through your head and notice the crown vibrating with energy. You may see or sense this energy of discernment flowing throughout your body. Allow it to do so, and then intend the discernment to return to your head and flow out your forehead and the back of your head to your bubble. As the energy flows back to you from your bubble, you may get an image, sensation or knowing of your core self within your body and your energy field. You might sense other energies flowing through your system that are different from your core energy. You might remember the words of other people or memories of their emotions. If you like, you can ask your natural energy defenses to dissolve, resolve and release any of those energies that conflict with your highest good. From your detached vantage point, see, feel or experience your natural energy defenses surround and release those energies. If this is challenging, just focus on the love flowing into your system from the earth and know that it is fueling the clearing process. If you like, you can also ask your natural energy defenses to help you process and release your own emotions related to what you released from other people. When this is all complete, it is time to move on to your final gift.

Now it's time to try out self-love. Pick an area of your life that needs more love. Imagine that you could see, feel or experience your heart space, the energetic home of your heart, in the middle of your chest. Imagine that one part of your heartspace is home to that issue in your life. Make the intention that self-love flows to that area. Know that even if you want love from other people to flow into this area, you need to fill it with self-love first, before any other love will flow in. If this is hard for you, ask your natural energy defenses to resolve, dissolve and release any energies that block this self-love. Ask your inner wisdom to teach you anything you need to know in order to release these blocks. As this healing occurs, you might notice that the authority and discernment energies are still flowing, and they support the healing. Notice the self-love energy flowing to you, filling your heart and then extend out of your heart, in front and back, to your bubble. You might also notice that the pendant is a magnet for self-love, drawing it into your body and heart. Allow the pendant to do this. As your heart fills with more and more self-love, feel free to intend and allow this love to flow deep into your heartspace, where your soul resides. If you need healing there, ask your inner wisdom and natural energy defenses to help you. Notice too that the self-love energy is quite healing. As these energies flow, you may notice areas or feelings of neediness relax. You may notice toxic connections to others naturally fall away and a deeper sense of safety within your being and your life. Notice how, when your heart is full of self-love, the area of your life that you want to improve may feel different or seem different. As this flow continues, you may get intuitive messages about what you can do to add more love into this area. You may realize that you need to learn more in order to act on that intuition. If so, ask the crystal to teach you how to take the actions suggested by your intuition. If you have no intuitive messages, just enjoy the flow of love. See, feel or experience how that love feels or changes as it flows.

Now take all of the energies of authority, discernment, self-love, self-discovery and healing and allow them to flow down through your body and into the earth. They flow, down, down, down to the place where you connect with earth energies. Allow these energies to fill this space and allow the earth energies to synthesize with them. As they integrate and synthesize, they become more real to you. Now allow these integrated energies to return to you. As you allow them to flow back up through the earth and into your body and your bubble, you might notice how much easier it is to feel your authority or discernment or self-love.

Now it's time to come back to the room and back to your chair, but before you do, let's remember all that you have done. You remember returning to the castle and spire. You remember the scepter, crown and pendant. You remember saying no and yes through your throat with authority energy and how that energy interacted with your bubble and your body. You remember discernment being drawn into you from your crown and how it helped you understand the difference between your own energy and other energies that do not belong to you. You remember how your natural energy defenses removed energies that did not serve your highest good. You also remember how the self-love poured from the pendant, into your heart and how you could channel that self-love into areas of your life that need more love. And finally, you remember how it felt to ground those energies and receive the integrated energy from the earth, allowing you to claim the authority, discernment and self-love as your own.

Now it's time to come back to your room and back to your chair. Turn your attention to your body seated in your chair.

Breathe deeply. Move your toes. Move your fingers. Take a deep breath, and when you are ready, open your eyes.

Second Bonus Section

If you feel that you are blocked in your authority or the authority energy did not flow freely, you could have attachments that interfere with the balanced, healthy flow of your personal authority energy. In this section, we will address the type of attachment that I call "hanging attachments." These are the types of energetic connections we might make when we hang on other people energetically. In doing so, we give up some of our responsibility for ourselves and put it on other people, institutions, movements or philosophies. When we make this kind of hanging attachment, we give up our authority and our power. This has a strong impact on your ability to hold your energetic space.

On the other hand, you can also allow others to create hanging attachments with or on you. In this kind of attachment, you energetically take on the responsibility for others. In doing so, you manage their power and authority in some area of their life.

Notice that in some circumstances this is normal and natural. We give up some authority over our income to the government so that we can live in a society. As workers, we do not have authority over our time. Parents with small children manage their authority until the children are able to manage it on their own. Physically or mentally impaired people may have to give up some of their power and authority to caregivers. As you might expect, these are great opportunities for growth and learning for all concerned. As we learn how to know the difference between healthy attachments and the dysfunctional, hanging attachments, we are more free to see and make choices that reflect who you are or who you want to be.

This meditation is meant to help you find and release the dysfunctional hanging attachments. First, you will learn how to get ready or be ready to release the dysfunctional attachments.

Second, you will use your discernment to see the difference between your own energy and the energies of these attachments. Third, you will allow your natural energy defenses to dissolve, resolve and release the attachments. Fourth, you will learn how to use your authority and your power in ways that create integrity and safety. Finally, you will learn how to live without the hanging attachments in your life.

Second Bonus Meditation

Find a place to sit and relax. Make sure you have this special time all to yourself and close your eyes. As you breathe in, take a moment to relax your body. Relax your lower body, allowing the chair to support you. Relax your upper body, letting your arms be soft and limp, your shoulders drop and your cheeks, scalp and neck melt and be still. Feel the gentle rise and fall of your chest. Now turn your imagination to the castle with its spire and the room at the top of the spire where you easily connect to your own inner wisdom. See and sense the scepter, crown and pendant. Notice how they support and assist you in using your authority, discernment and self-love.

Now, ask your inner wisdom to help you get ready and be ready to release any dysfunctional hanging attachments from your energy field and your experience. Know and accept that your inner wisdom may be adjusting your beliefs and perceptions or dissolving past agreements or oaths so that you understand how to have more healthy energetic relations. See, feel or experience the wisdom energy flow through your whole body and your whole being. It goes through your past, present and future and the parts of you that are not in the flow of time. It goes to your soul and your genetic connections to those who have come before you. It goes to all of your sensations and all of your energy. As it does so, it prepares you to easily and gently release unhealthy attachments. Now allow the energy of this learning to flow down through your body and ground into the earth where it can mix and mingle with earth energies. When the integration of the energy is complete, allow the integrated energy to return to you, your body and the bubble that surrounds you.

Now use your authority and discernment to find the dysfunctional attachments. Tap the floor three times with the scepter and make the intention to discern the attachments that interfere with the flow of your authority. See, feel or experience the energies of authority and discernment flowing to and through you. See the gem in the scepter blaze with light. Feel the crown vibrate with the energy of discernment and allow yourself to see or sense the unhealthy attachments. Now ask your natural energy defenses to dissolve, resolve and release these attachments and any difficult or unhealthy emotions or sensations that relate to them. Watch, experience or know that the attachments are leaving your system. Notice how as you relax and allow, the release becomes easier and more complete. You may want to focus on the authority and discernment energies flowing in through your head and feet. Or you may begin to naturally feel the flow of self-love or love from your natural energy defenses come and fill in the vacant areas. Now let all that healing and all of those changes ground down to the earth. When they have integrated and synthesized with earth energies, allow the integrated energies to return to you, your body and the bubble that surrounds you.

Now ask your inner wisdom to teach you how to use your authority and your power in ways that create integrity and safety without unhealthy attachments in your life. See, feel or experience the energy of wisdom come down into your head, filling your mind, your body, your heart and your gut. You see it fill up all time and no time. It fills your soul and your genetic blueprint. You see it permeate your whole bubble. Allow your inner wisdom to readjust your beliefs and perspectives in ways that help you know at the deepest levels how to use and manage your energies in these new and healthy ways. As you do so, you may feel or sense your life or your energy field expanding in ways that leave you feeling safer, more relaxed and at home in your being or body. Again, you allow the wisdom to ground down into the earth, knowing that as the wisdom integrates with the earth, you more deeply claim the learning and integrate it into your being. Allow the integrated energy to return to your and your bubble. Take a moment to sit in this new understanding and easier energy. Now initiate the flow or your authority energy. Use this energy to intend to live without the dysfunctional hanging attachments and see the authority energy flow to and through you and fill up your bubble.

Now it's time to come back to your body and back to your current time and place, but before you do, let's remember all that you have done. You remember the castle, the scepter, the crown and the pendant. You remember what it meant and how it felt to get ready to release unhealthy attachments. You remember using your authority and discernment to identify and release those attachments and what it felt like to allow your natural energy defenses to dissolve them and replace them with love. You may have also felt your own self-love flow to those spaces and fill them up. And you remember learning how to live safely and with integrity without the dysfunctional attachments. And finally, you remember using your authority to establish new ways of being that assure healthier and better uses of your authority and power.

So now come back to your room, back to your chair and back to your body. Feel your feet on the floor. Wriggle your toes. Move your fingers. Move your shoulders, and when you are ready, take a deep breath and open your eyes.

Exercise 16: General Health

In this section, we will touch lightly on the issue of general health. It is a wide topic, holding much potential for learning and growth. The imagery exercise in this section provides a metaphor that is intended to help you access balanced, easy, healing energies and circulate them through your system. It is not meant to give you magical or miraculous healings. If you have a medical condition, seek medical help. This meditation will supplement your treatment and support your best outcomes. If instead, you feel a lack of vitality or want to explore new techniques to enhance your experience of good health, you may enjoy the following.

Grounding Meditation

Do this meditation seated in a chair, with your feet flat on the floor. If you like, you can lay down during the meditation, but if you find yourself falling asleep, you may choose to sit while doing these meditations. Always intend that your meditations be gentle, balanced and healthy for you. Please note that the following meditations include requests or intentions for learning and healing. You do not have to repeat each request or intention in full. Instead, when you read or hear the suggested intention or request, simply say to yourself, "Yes, I intend that."

Take a deep breath and close your eyes. Now take a moment and imagine that you are in a lovely, immense, walled garden. You might see flowers, bushes, vegetables, hedges or even statues or structures. Turn your attention to the center of the garden where you see a big and beautiful tree. The tree stretches much higher than the wall, and its branches are wide and strong. As you get near the tree you see soft green grass at the base of the tree. Go ahead and sit down with your back resting on the trunk of the tree. Feel the vibrant cool grass beneath you, giving you a perfect cushion and the comforting support of the trunk against your back. As you close your eyes, you begin to fall in tune with the tree. You begin to sense its life and energy. It's almost as if you can detect the sap flowing up and down within the structure of the tree, its strength and flexibility as it easily moves with the breeze and how it gives a home to other creatures along its limbs. As you breathe deeply, you begin to sink into the tree and become the tree. You notice that your roots are deep and wide, as if your feet and toes are sunk into the cool, welcoming earth. You feel your strong boughs stretching out and up to the sky and your leaves or needles drinking in nourishment from the sun. You feel delicious goodness beaming and pouring onto you and you take it in like food or air or an embrace from a beloved. You breathe through your leaves and you drink through your roots. And it all happens in a natural choreographed dance of nature as you sway to the rhythm of the breeze. Feel your glory, your strength, your height and depth and the vitality that moves to you and through you. Take a moment to enjoy these sensations, and when you are ready, come back to the room, open your eyes and take a deep breath.

Imagery Meditation

Close your eyes and again return to the garden, to the tree and your experience of becoming the tree. Again, become one with the tree. Explore your roots. Notice how the soil is strong enough to hold you firm and safe, but porous enough to let in oxygen and water. Notice that the water has dissolved just the right amount of nutrients to bring you everything you need to be healthy and strong. Drink in the nutritious water and the life giving oxygen. Feel your whole root structure, as wide and deep as you are tall and wide, drink, absorb and receive from the earth. As you do so, you notice that as you drink in these life giving nutrients, earth energy flows into your system. Really feel your roots and the tickling or buzzing sensation of the earth energy flowing there. Feel how the water, the nutrients, the oxygen and the energy bring strength, vitality and calm. Feel how good it feels to dig your roots into the earth and how the earth so abundantly brings you more than enough life, health and vitality. You revel in the vitality, an ever flowing system of renewal.

The water and nutrients and energy rise up through the roots into the trunk of the tree. You see and experience the multitude of pathways that bring all this goodness into the trunk of the tree, expanding out to the bark and up into the limbs, twigs, needles or leaves. The goodness goes into your cells and molecules where you see, feel and experience sunlight, like an engine of energy. You feel this engine turning like a waterwheel, bringing you more vitality. So much vitality in each needle or leaf. So much so that it must overflow or slip down into the twigs, branches, trunk and roots. So much so that it must expand out of the leaves or needles. The engine of vitality is so powerful and abundant that it must go downward to the whole of the tree and all excess goes outward in all directions. Notice now that you, as the tree, have a bubble that surrounds you, with natural energy defenses within the bubble and within each part of the tree. You feel or see how the natural energy defenses bring the right kind of balance so that you use the exact right energy to be strong and healthy, both above and below ground. Take a moment and feel the balance that these natural energy defenses bring both above and below ground. Notice that as you allow these defenses to work for you, it is easier to simply relax and enjoy all of these natural, abundant processes to work and allow you to feel the health and vitality. As you relax and enjoy, you might notice how busy your system is, drinking in goodness, breathing in goodness, allowing the engine of photosynthesis to work and create, circulating nutrients, energies and health. You notice the busyness of your natural energy defenses, both within your tree structure and within the bubble that surrounds you. You notice how good it feels to let go of any excess vitality and how there is always more than enough goodness, always more than enough for your growth and your balance.

Now it's time to step out of the tree. As your awareness begins to pull itself inward, it goes in toward the trunk. You begin to see yourself at the base of the tree, leaning against the trunk. You intend and allow your awareness to return back into your body, and you bring with you the memories and sensations of vitality and the engine of energy. Your consciousness is now wholly in your body as you are still sitting at the base of the tree. Now you get up and thank the tree for all you have experienced and learned, and you step away from the tree and away from the bubble that surrounds it.

Find a place in the sunshine where you can stand and open your arms wide, just like the limbs of the tree. Imagine that your energy roots extend down into the earth and that your fingers, hands and arms could synthesize energy from the sun. Imagine that you could take all the nutrients and earth energies you need up through your energy roots, circulating all of that goodness to your entire body and the bubble that surrounds you. Notice the abundance of goodness, both coming up through your roots, into your feet, legs and body and coming down through your hands, arms, head and body. Notice how these energies relax your shoulders, neck and back. Notice how the vitality relaxes your whole body. Notice areas of tension, discomfort or dysfunction drink in the vitality. Notice the engine of goodness in both of your hands, in your right hand, and in your left hand. And notice that if there is any imbalance, your natural energy defenses bring balance and security there. See, feel or experience your natural energy defenses within your body. They flow beneath your skin, around each organ, around each muscle, around each bone and joint, around your whole head, brain, eyes, ears, nose and mouth. They surround all of you and all of your roots and all of your bubble. Make the intention that your natural energy defenses are more real than anything that brings imbalance. If you like, you can ask your inner wisdom to teach you how to experience this new truth and reality. Allow your natural energy defenses and engine and system of vitality to be your reality and your truth.

Now allow your natural energy defenses and your engine and system of vitality to repair or restructure anything that needs new life, new structure or repair. You may see, feel or experience specific areas of your body regenerate or rebalance. You may see images or symbols of genes being switched on or off. You may imagine areas of your energetic environment cleansing or balancing which will automatically make positive changes to your body and your health. You may experience calming or cleansing of your mind or mental processes or your emotional processes. Or you may just relax and enjoy the circulation of vitality and goodness, reveling in the reality of your health and vitality.

Now ask your inner wisdom or higher power to teach you anything else you need to know about your health. Let that information wash through your whole being, mind, heart, gut, time and soul. Now allow the energy to flow to the earth, integrate and return to you and your bubble. Take a moment to enjoy the energies of health and vitality flowing through your system.

Now it's time to return to your room and return to your chair, but before you do, let's remember all that you have done. You remember the garden with its tree. You remember becoming the tree and your roots in the earth. You remember the flowing system of renewal and how the sunlight fueled the engine of vitality so abundantly, that some of those vital energies had to overflow out to the earth and how good that felt. You remember stepping out of the tree and becoming yourself again. You remember taking the experiences of the tree in ways that allowed you to extend your energy roots into the earth and absorb sunshine through your fingers and hands. You remember the abundance of goodness flowing into you through your roots and in through your hands and arms. You remember the nutrients flowing to you and specific areas drinking them in and becoming satiated. You remember the relaxation that you felt and the healing and balancing coming from your natural energy defenses. You remember how your natural energy defenses surrounded every part of you, your skin, your organs, your muscles and bones, your head, all of your senses and all of your roots and your bubble. You remember the regeneration, rebalancing and cleansing of mind, body and emotions. You remember how good all of this felt and the reality of your health and vitality.

Now it's time to come back to your room and back to your chair. Feel your body. Feel your breath. Feel yourself seated in your chair and your feet on the floor. Move your body. When you are ready, take a deep breath and open your eyes.

Follow up questions

What did your tree look like and what did it feel like to be the tree?

What did it feel like to grow energy roots into the earth?

What part or parts were easy and what parts were hard? Are there areas that need more balancing or healing? If so, what?

Describe what you felt with the vitality and health flowing through your system.

Did this help you feel safer? Please describe.

Exercise 17: Infectious Disease

I begin my comments about this exercise with the same proviso I mentioned previously. Please do not mistake this imagery for some kind of magical protection against disease. One truth that I have seen over and over again is the necessity to use both energy and action to be healthy and balanced. If you try to build energetic defenses on the one hand and at the same time take actions or fail to take other actions that put you at risk for disease, you block or destroy your energetic defenses. On the other hand, if you rely only on actions to keep you safe, I believe you leach energetic power from your ability to live in good health and safety from disease. When you take safety precautions that are reasonable and combine them with self-care and energy that is fueled by love and guided by wisdom, you are using your personal power in a balanced and healthy way.

Grounding Meditation

Do this meditation seated in a chair, with your feet flat on the floor. If you like, you can lay down during the meditation, but if you find yourself falling asleep, you may choose to sit while doing these meditations. Always intend that your meditations be gentle, balanced and healthy for you. Please note that the following meditations include requests or intentions for learning and healing. You do not have to repeat each request or intention in full. Instead, when you read or hear the suggested intention or request, simply say to yourself, "Yes, I intend that."

Take a deep breath and close your eyes. Return to your garden and your tree of health. Take a moment to enjoy the energies you feel while you are near your tree. And now you decide to wander and explore the garden a little bit more. You might see areas of flowers or vegetables or fruit trees. You might see mysterious pathways or more formal plantings. As you wander, you realize that this is your garden, a place where you can return at any time to explore and enjoy, But now it's time to find a special place in your garden. This is a place where the earth gives you a very precious gift. Take a moment to look around. See a place with an outcropping of large boulders. As you approach this place, you notice that the air becomes damper, cooler. As you reach the boulders, you touch one and feel its coolness, as if it is bringing up the steady, constant ground temperature. It is a perfect contrast to the warmth of the sun. As you pick your way around these boulders, you see a depression in one of them that contains crystalline, pure water. You see that it is fed by a small trickle of a tiny spring. This water smells clean and feels clean as you breathe in its scents. And now, all of a sudden, you begin to experience a kind of x-ray vision, as if your eyes become able to focus like a very strong microscope. As you look, you see that this water is filled with tiny, tiny microbes. They are smaller than bacteria, smaller than a virus, smaller than the cells of your body. As your eyes focus, you see that these squiggling creatures all have miniature scissor-like appendages. You realize that they are different, very different from anything you have ever seen before, and you know that they are very special and precious. You feel the anticipation of learning more about them and what they can do for you. You know that with this water, containing these microbes, your body is safe from infectious disease. Take a moment to feel the safety, relief and gratitude for this gift. Now, come back to the room, take a deep breath, and open your eyes.

Imagery Meditation

Close your eyes. And now return to your garden, and return to the place where the tiny spring feeds that small pool of crystalline water. Again, your x-ray vision sees the trillions and trillions of microbes within the water. You find that there is a small cup there, perfectly sized to scoop up some of the water. So you do. You scoop some of the water into the cup, and you hold it high above your head. As you hold the water up to the sunlight, ask the sunlight to charge or program these microbes to find and to cut the genetic structure of the infectious disease that is in your body now or that may, in the future, try to attack your body. If you like, you can name the disease that you want targeted. Or in the alternative, you can name the symptoms that you want alleviated, such as, "Whatever disease that is causing my experience of [fill in the blank], please program the microbes to target and remove the disease." As the sunlight begins to charge and program the microbes, it's as if the microbes turn to the sun and absorb its energy and its directives. It may seem as if the microbes are listening or filling up or transforming. When this is complete, you lower the cup and drink the crystalline water. Your x-ray vision allows you to see the water and the trillions of microbes flow into your stomach and digestive system, into your bloodstream where they speed to the infectious disease. They are tiny compared to the bacteria or virus, but they swarm the disease and are so small that they easily slip inside the disease and into the genetic structure of the disease itself. These microbes find the special place within the DNA of the disease and cut it. The DNA, which is tightly coiled, immediately unravels, springing apart. You watch as the disease falls apart, disintegrates. Without its DNA blueprint, it cannot be. Now you watch as millions, countless numbers of invading virus or bacteria fall apart, rupture and turn into particles of nothingness. Your body easily washes them away, out and away, gone forever.

And now, the microbes easily and naturally merge with the energy of your natural energy defenses. These defenses instantly and naturally know how to increase the security in your body's cells. Use your x-ray vision and see your natural energy defenses go to all of the cells of your body and find places where infectious disease tries to attach. Watch as your natural energy defenses upgrade the security by covering those attachment spots and putting in place new ways of operating so that nutrients and goodness easily flow in, but invading disease can find no place to latch on. You might see, feel or experience each cell in your body glowing or vibrating with light and goodness. And you know that any future disease will be blocked. Now you feel your whole being filled with beautiful light and high vibration. Feel how it relaxes you, and at the same time fills you with wellbeing. Allow yourself to revel in the wondrous feeling of safety and ease.

Now it's time to come back to your room and back to your chair, but before you do, let's remember all that you have done. You remember your garden, with its tree of health and all of the interesting things to find and explore there. You remember the outcropping of boulders and the spring and small well of crystalline water. You remember observing the microbes and scooping them into the cup and how the sunlight charged and programmed the microbes to target infectious disease. You remember drinking the water and how the microbes were able to speed to the disease, swarm it and cut its DNA. You remember how the disease fell apart and washed away. You also remember how your natural energy defenses learned how to upgrade the security of your cells, and how your cells easily adopted the new security and began to glow with new health and energy. You remember how the disease with its lower vibration cannot come close to the healthy, vibrating cells of your body.

Now it's time to come back to your room, back to your chair, and back to your body. Take a nice deep breath, move your body. Wiggle your toes, move your fingers, and in your own time, open your eyes.

Follow up questions

What did the healing microbes look like to you?

Describe what you saw when the microbes cut the DNA of the disease.

What did you see or experience when your cells got a security upgrade?

If you think about infectious disease, how do you feel?

Did this help you feel safer? Please describe.

Exercise 18: Sexuality

Sexuality in our culture is the oddest thing. Culture is saturated with sexual references. Popular music, dance, movies, etc. fill the airwaves with descriptions and depictions of sexuality that run the gamut from the depraved to the sublime. At the same time, it is difficult for people to speak openly about sexuality and all of the ways in which individuals may need healing, growth, wisdom or just plain kindness or love in their experiences of their sexual selves. This imagery meditation will use a body scanning technique of healing. You will sense your whole energetic system of sexuality and any areas of dysfunction, energy leaks or areas that might be enhanced by new knowledge. As some people may have multiple areas of potential learning, you may find that you need to take each dysfunction or lack one by one. If you need to do this exercise multiple times, know that each healing adds to your empowerment, safety and enjoyment of this vital part of life.

WARNING: I use anatomical terms for sexual organs in this meditation. If you find this embarrassing or inflammatory, please remember that we all have sexual organs, they are natural, and it's okay to talk about them.

Grounding Meditation

Do this meditation seated in a chair, with your feet flat on the floor. If you like, you can lay down during the meditation, but if you find yourself falling asleep, you may choose to sit while doing these meditations. Always intend that your meditations be gentle, balanced and healthy for you. Please note that the following meditations include requests or intentions for learning and healing. You do not have to repeat each request or intention in full. Instead, when you read or hear the suggested intention or request, simply say to yourself, "Yes, I intend that."

Take a deep breath and close your eyes. Allow yourself to relax into your chair. Let your body be heavy. Feel your feet against the floor. Allow your arms and shoulders to relax even more. Let your scalp, face and neck soften. Now imagine that with your eyes closed, you could see a screen in front of you. On that screen, you see a silhouette of your body. It might look like a line drawing. Within this silhouette, you see lines of bright color running throughout the body, head to toe, fingers to shoulders with brighter, thicker columns running from your head to the base of your torso. You might also see bright circles of light along those columns along with finer, filigree patterns or systems of light. This is your body's life force energy system.

Now make the intention to hone in and see or experience the energy system of your sexuality. You might see lines of light or color, or you might see shapes or symbols that represent that system. You might have knowings or find some clarity about the energetics of your sexuality. Whatever you experience, explore it by getting close to the image or allow yourself to more deeply experience the knowing or message. Pay attention to what you feel as you connect with the energetics of your sexuality. Now take a moment to thank the color or symbol or knowing for the information you have gathered. Now, come back to the room, open your eyes and take a deep breath.

Imagery Meditation

Close your eyes. You might notice that by simply putting your attention on your sexuality and its system of energy, you have difficult emotions wanting to flow out and away. If so, ask your natural energy defenses to help you with the process of releasing emotion with ease and in ways that feel safe. If these emotions are too challenging, you know that you can stop at any time, take a breather or come back to this meditation at another time. In addition, you can turn down the intensity of the emotion by imagining that you have a dial and knob that you can turn. As you turn the knob to the left, the intensity decreases. As you turn the knob to the right, the flow increases. Focus on your natural energy defenses. See or feel how they break up difficult emotional energy and help it wash away. Your focus helps guide your natural energy defenses. As you focus on an area, your natural energy defenses rush in there, bringing balance and healing. Focus on the images and sensations of balance and health from your natural energy defenses. You might also see the silhouette on the screen with your natural energy defenses surrounding the silhouette, bathing it in the loving, safe energy from the earth. In addition, if you feel as if your system of sexual energy is under attack, ask your inner wisdom to teach your natural energy defenses how to upgrade the security of your bubble so that goodness can flow in, but attack energy is repelled.

When you feel ready to know more, it's time for us to make sure that what you are seeing and experiencing is your own energy of sexuality. You can always, at a later time, allow other sexual energies into your system, but for right now, this is your time to explore your own system of sexuality. Make the intention that your natural energy defenses remove any sexual energies that do not belong to you. If you want this to operate for a limited time frame, make sure to intend that. If you like, you can ask your inner wisdom to adjust your beliefs and give you the knowledge that will help you to release all sexual energies that do not belong to you and discern the difference between your sexual system of energy and the energies of others. Allow the energy of healing and wisdom in through your head, into your mind, heart and gut. Allow it to flow through all time and no time, including the present time. Allow it into your soul and into your genetic blueprint. Now let it flow down to the earth where you connect to earth energies, and let the earth synthesize and integrate these energies and return the integrated energy to you and your bubble. Notice that as you release the non-you energies, your natural energy defenses fill in the spaces with beautiful love energy. This is the pure, clean energy of the earth.

Now ask your inner wisdom to retune your beliefs and perspectives to healthy ones and teach you anything you need to know about your own sexuality, its energetic system and your experience of pleasure, letting this wisdom flow to your mind, heart, gut, soul, all time and no time. It goes deeply into your body and its genetic structure. Ground the wisdom into the earth and let the integrated energies return to you and your bubble. Now turn your attention to the screen in front of you. Make the intention to see your own energetic system of sexuality. You might see it in one or many spaces or throughout the whole body. Now make the intention to see a red *X* over any part of your sexual energetic system that needs healing. You may have more than one area of need, but for now, intend to see the area that needs attention today. Imagine that you could zero in on that area of the *X*. Ask your inner wisdom what you need to know or what needs to change in order for that area to become healthy and whole. You may immediately receive a knowing or message. If not, imagine that the energy of the answer flows into your whole being from your inner wisdom or higher power. Go ahead and ground the energy of the answer and let it return to you and your bubble. Now ask your inner wisdom or higher power to again retune your beliefs and perspectives in order to make those changes easy, safe and fulfilling. Again, you allow these changes through your whole being, grounding these energies and allowing the integrated energies to fill you and your bubble.

Now ask your inner wisdom or higher power to teach you how to let more goodness and pleasure into your sexuality and your energetic system of sexuality, adjusting beliefs or perspectives, if needed. Once more you allow this wisdom to fill your whole being, you ground it and you accept the integrated, synthesized earth energy into your body and your bubble. Turn your attention back to the screen in front of you. Intend to see the energies of safety, balance and permission to feel pleasure fill your sexuality. Let it fill your genitals. If you are a woman, let it into your clitoris and vulva. Let it into your vagina, cervix and reproductive organs. If you are a man, allow the energies of safety, balance and permission to feel pleasure into your prostate, testicles and penis and all of the structures that connect and support them. Now, regardless of gender, allow these energies and permission to expand to other parts of your body, and all of your senses. You may feel as if these pleasant, safe energies are washing out old sensations from your nervous system, creating a new order of goodness, security and pleasure. You may feel as if these energies are upgrading your sexuality, enhancing it, making it more precious, more deeply fulfilling and more abundant in your life. Now allow these energies to expand to your inner being, the you inside. Let your inner being be filled with sexual safety, sexual balance and the permission to feel sexual pleasure. If you like, ask your inner wisdom to teach you what you need to know about the connection between these beautiful energies and love. Now it's time to ground all of the safety, all of the goodness, all of the pleasure and all of the wisdom down into the earth. Take a moment to experience what it feels like to let these energies integrate and synthesize with earth energies. Now allow the integrated energies back up into your body and into the bubble that surrounds you. Take a moment to enjoy these energies.

Now it's time to come back to your room and back to your chair, but before you do, let's remember all that we have done. You remember the screen in front of you with your silhouette. You remember seeing your energy systems and seeing or connecting with your sexuality's energy system. You remember the cleansing of old emotion and releasing energies that do not belong to you from this energy system of your sexuality. And you remember how those spaces were filled with loving earth energy. You remember learning and accepting new, healthy beliefs about your sexuality and finding specific areas that need healing. You watched as wisdom and healing flowed to that area, and you learned about changes you may need to make. You learned how to allow in more goodness, safety and permission for pleasure into your sexuality, watching it flow into your genitals, your body, all your senses and to your inner being. And you may also have accepted new wisdom about the connections between love, pleasure, balance and safety.

Now it's time to come back to your room and back to your chair. Feel yourself within your body. Move your fingers. Move your toes. Shrug your shoulders. Take a deep breath, and in your own time, open your eyes.

Follow up questions

What about this meditation surprised you?

Are there areas of your sexuality that still need healing or growth? If so, what, and what do you plan to do to further or support this healing or growth?

What part or parts were easy and what parts were hard?

How do you feel about pleasure, and has that changed because of the meditation?

Did this help you feel safer? Please describe.

Exercise 19: Money, Success, Reputation

You might wonder what this subject is doing in a book about energy defenses that are guided by wisdom and fueled by love. Maybe you think that money, success and reputation are too materialistic or selfish or even corrupt for your inner wisdom or a system that depends on love. Perhaps you think that money or success cancel out love or wisdom. Perhaps you just feel rotten when you think about money, success or reputation. If you are feeling these reservations or others, you might be the exact person who benefits most from this meditation.

I believe that love and wisdom make everything better in all ways, even when it comes to financial security, success and reputation. What I mean by better is that it becomes more synced up with a higher perspective of good, removing artificial limitations such as, "I can't be spiritual or worthy and financially secure." or "I must choose between success and what is most important to me." Imagine that you could take your "self" out of the way of the flow of goodness. Wouldn't the flow of goodness need a balanced and healthy financial foundation in order to be able to flow out into the world and make a positive difference? Isn't success necessary or inevitable in order for goodness to reach others? How can others trust the flow of goodness without a good reputation? The trick to all of this is to know the difference between inner nonsense and inner wisdom and to have the courage to follow the wisdom. Sometimes it comes down to feeling the fear and doing it anyway, knowing that the outcome will be goodness for others along with your growth as a conscious being. And, if along the way, your financial security, success and reputation grow in a way that is pleasing to you, know that goodness makes everything better, including your pleasure, security and joy in the work that you do.

Grounding Meditation

Do this meditation seated in a chair, with your feet flat on the floor. If you like, you can lay down during the meditation, but if you find yourself falling asleep, you may choose to sit while doing these meditations. Always intend that your meditations be gentle, balanced and healthy for you. Please note that the following meditations include requests or intentions for learning and healing. You do not have to repeat each request or intention in full. Instead, when you read or hear the suggested intention or request, simply say to yourself, "Yes, I intend that."

Take a deep breath and close your eyes. Take a moment to tune into the newness of each moment. See, feel or experience how each heartbeat is different from the one before. The mixture of the air is different with each breath. The angle of the sun is different. The pull of the tides change with each breath and each heartbeat. And the newness of the energy is constantly flowing to and through you. This is what it is like to be a child. Now imagine being a child. You are a child in a sandbox. As you sit in your sandbox, you are also in a bubble that surrounds and protects you. This bubble is grounded into the earth and into that place where you as a child connect with earth energy. Now begin to make something with the sand. Feel the coolness and texture of the sand and form something. As you do, see, feel or experience the energy of inspiration flowing into your head, down your body and into your hands. See, feel or experience love from the earth coming up into your body, mixing with the inspiration and flowing out of your hands to create something with the sand. See, feel or experience the earth energies and the intuitive energies in and around your creation. You may also see something of yourself within your creation, as if the investment of your time and focus has given this creation a certain scent or flavor of the very best of you. Now allow your natural energy defenses to surround and protect this creation. This protection is fueled by earth energy. If you see, feel or experience any cords or connections of energy between you and your creation, ask your natural energy defenses to dissolve, resolve and release these cords. See the creation naturally form its own bubble, separate from yours, and its connection to the earth is now fueled by its own grounding cord. As you turn your attention back to your natural energy defenses and the bubble that surrounds you, you may see your creation release away from you or change in some way. As this happens, see, feel or experience the flow of goodness from the earth to you grow or become richer or more wondrous. Notice the difference between your creation, how it changes or where it goes and your energy, your experience and your ability to send positive life force energy from the earth to any part of your being, including the parts of your being that are responsible for your physical abundance, success or reputation. See the difference in the energy of your creation and your energetic system and its robust flow of goodness. Now, come back to the room, open your eyes and take a deep breath.

Imagery Meditation

Close your eyes. Return to that awareness of the newness of each moment. Let the newness from earth energies flow into your feet, up your legs, into your body, shoulders, arms and head. See, feel or experience the bubble that surrounds you filling up with the energies and the flow of newness. Now turn your attention to your imagination, and imagine that you are out in space, surrounded by your protective bubble and your natural energy defenses. Know that you are grounded and that your natural energy defenses are fueled by love. Know that you are easily and naturally connected to your inner wisdom.

Ask your inner wisdom to show you the part of your energy system responsible for your physical abundance. You see it on a screen in front of you or simply see, feel or experience something that represents your abundance system. This abundance system facilitates the flow of money or resources that create your financial security. It might be in your body or in the energy field that surrounds you. Or you might see or experience a shape or something else that represents this entire system. If it looks beautiful or not beautiful, it is okay. Know that it is growing and changing and that love and wisdom will bring goodness to this system. Ask your inner wisdom to teach you what you need to know about this system and teach your natural energy defenses how to protect this system and balance it. If you like, you can ask your inner wisdom to readjust your beliefs so that you believe you deserve wealth and financial security. See, feel or experience the wisdom energy flow to your whole system, mind, heart, gut, backward and forward through time, to the present and to no time, and to your soul and genetic blueprint.

If you are feeling fear or some other unpleasant emotion, make the request that the energies of these emotions dissolve, resolve and release. As you experience the flows of these energies, you may see or experience changes in your system of physical abundance. This is fine. Just focus on the flow of wisdom to your whole self. Now ask your inner wisdom to teach or change your system of physical abundance in ways that generate good for you and win-win outcomes for all concerned, releasing beliefs or energies that block the flow of goodness. Again, allow this wisdom energy into your whole being, to your mind, heart, gut and soul. It goes to all of time and experiences of no time as well as all of your genetic material.

Now ground all of these energies into the earth. All of these energies flow down to the earth, down to that place within the earth where you connect your being to the beautiful, positive earth energies. See, feel or experience the earth energies merge with the learning, healing and wisdom. Experience or know that this merging integrates and synthesizes these energies so that you can incorporate the wisdom into your life. Now, allow the integrated and synthesized energies to flow back up to you, filling your body and the bubble that surrounds you.

Now we will repeat all of this learning, healing and growth with the energies of success and reputation. You are still in space, in your bubble, grounded, protected and fueled by love and wisdom. Make the intention to see the system within you that is responsible for success. Remember that the energies that fuel this success are wisdom and inspiration from your higher power or inner wisdom and love and goodness from the earth. Ask your inner wisdom to adjust your beliefs and perspectives to allow the good to flow through this system of success in ways that are balanced, healthy and in the highest good of all concerned. Ask your inner wisdom or higher power to teach you and your natural energy defenses to allow more protection of your success and the good that it brings to the world. Allow all of this learning and all of these changes into your whole being. As you allow these energies to flow forward and backward through your heart, you also see it go in all directions into the present and deep within your heart to your soul and deep into the smallest particles of your physical being. These energies flow down, down, down, through your body and into the earth to that place where you connect to the earth and you allow this connection to integrate, synthesize and change these energies so that they belong to you. You claim these energies by allowing them to flow up through your grounding cord, up into your body, filling your body and the bubble that surrounds you. Now check in with your energy system of success. Allow these earth energies to flow through that system. They go through that system and out into your bubble. Notice that you don't have to send energies into your bubble. Instead, you allow the energies to flow naturally.

Turn your attention again to the image, sensations or knowings of you, protected and grounded out in space, in your bubble, connected to your flow of inner wisdom. Ask your inner wisdom or higher power to teach you and your natural energy defenses what you need to know about your reputation and its protection. If you like, you can ask your inner wisdom to adjust or change your beliefs and perspectives to help you know that you deserve goodness, love and protection in your reputation. Again you allow all of this learning and all of these changes into your whole being. Now ask your inner wisdom to show you your energetic system of your reputation. See the image, feel the sensations or experience the knowing. Ask your inner wisdom or higher power to heal anything that needs positive change within this system and teach you anything else you may need to know to allow yourself to experience a healthy reputation, and one protected by your natural energy defenses. After allowing all of these energies into your whole being, throughout time and space, you ground those energies into the earth. Feel how the earth changes these energies, synchronizing them with your own energies, making them part of your being. Now you allow these synchronized energies flow back to you and back to the bubble that surrounds you. Check back in with your energy system of reputation. Really allow these earth energies to flow through this system and through your bubble. Check in with your natural energy defenses and see, feel or experience those defenses protecting this system.

Now let's try out these systems. Remember the experience of being a child in a sandbox, how the flows of inspiration and love combined to create something that resulted in its own bubble and grounding chord. Remember the fulfillment of allowing it release into the world and away from you. Let's try that again, using your systems of abundance, success and reputation. Imagine something that you would like to create as a worker, professional, caretaker, student or entrepreneur. It could be anything, from a solution to a problem to a new widget to a new job, artistic creation or more. Take a moment to see how this creation will help other people. Ask your inner wisdom and the earth to help you create this. Take a moment to allow the inspiration to flow from your inner wisdom and the love to flow from the earth to mix and mingle within you and flow out of you into the bubble in front of you. Watch it take shape in front of you. Your creation forms its own bubble and its own grounding cord. When it is complete, turn your attention to the flow of energy through your systems of abundance, success and reputation. Your creation moves out of your bubble and into the world, taking with it the good that funnelled through you. As you release your creation, focus on the deep energies of fulfillment, joy and satisfaction that wash through your systems of abundance, success and reputation. As the energies continue to flow through your abundance, success and reputation systems, those energies flow into your bubble to fill it with goodness. Notice that your natural energy defenses surround and protect your system of abundance, success and reputation and make sure that your bubble is completely intact and balanced.

Now it's time to come back to your room and back to your chair, but before you do, let's take a moment to remember all we have done. You remember the sandbox and your creation and you remember being out in space, in your bubble, grounded in the earth's love and protected by your natural energy defenses. You remember the energetic systems of physical abundance, success and reputation. You also remember how these systems healed or changed with the shifts in your own beliefs and perceptions and how your natural energy defenses surrounded and protected each of these energy systems. You remember what it felt like to claim the synthesized energies from the earth so that you could be more in sync with your natural affinity for abundance, success and reputation. You also remember what it felt like to create, using inspiration and love and how this loving gift to the world was released or expressed to the world through the positive energies that flow through your systems of abundance, success and reputation and how it all is naturally protected by your natural energy defenses.

Now it's time to come back to the room and back to your chair. Send your consciousness back to your body. Feel your body. Feel your weight against the chair. Feel your feet flat on the floor. Feel your breath moving in and out of your body. Move your body. Stretch. And when you are ready, take a deep breath and open your eyes.

Follow up questions

What changed in your understanding of money, success or reputation?

What insights, if any, did you receive about new ways of being in relation to your abundance, success or reputation?

What part or parts were easy and what parts were hard?

How do you feel about allowing your natural energy defenses to protect your abundance, success and reputation?

Did this help you feel safer? Please describe.

Exercise 20: Love

So many of these topics are rich with potential. So many of these topics could generate an entire book of exercises to bring balance and goodness. This is one of those topics. There is so much for us to learn about love, and there are so many types of love in this world for us to cultivate. One exercise will not encompass it all. So I offer a beginning, a way into this topic with the following exercise. I believe that love is not a possession, it is a force that, when you let it work on you, change you, love you, open you, free you, you achieve your highest purpose.

Grounding Meditation

Do this meditation seated in a chair, with your feet flat on the floor. If you like, you can lay down during the meditation, but if you find yourself falling asleep, you may choose to sit while doing these meditations. Always intend that your meditations be gentle, balanced and healthy for you. Please note that the following meditations include requests or intentions for learning and healing. You do not have to repeat each request or intention in full. Instead, when you read or hear the suggested intention or request, simply say to yourself, "Yes, I intend that."

Take a deep breath and close your eyes. Remember the garden with your tree of health. Go back there. Imagine yourself underneath the beautiful tree that resonates with health and vitality. Take a moment and drink in those energies of health and vitality. When you feel ready, we will explore and find the part of the garden that is dedicated to love. If you like, you can ask your inner wisdom to guide you there. This guidance might come in the form of a sign with an arrow, a feeling of pulling attraction or perhaps an animal or something else that you can follow to your garden of love. This garden of love is just one part of the bigger garden, but it is separated off with a hedge or fence or special plantings that allow you to see your garden of love as a lovely and unique creation. As you get close to your garden of love, you might see that some portions are teeming with life and others are less so. Or, you might see a well balanced garden. You might notice that some areas need healing or that others haven't even been planted yet. Whatever you see, it is perfect and good. Know that there is more than enough life, more than enough healing, more than enough guidance and goodness to make your garden of love a blessing to you. As you enter your garden of love, notice that each part of this garden relates to a different kind of love in your life. One area relates to family love, another contains love of self, another might be romantic love or spiritual love or love of a particular activity or type of experience. Notice how personal this garden is. Notice that what is planted here is about you and what you love and what you value and what you are learning about. This garden is yours and only yours. Take a moment and enjoy the energies of all that you love. Now, come back to the room, take a nice deep breath and open your eyes.

Imagery Meditation

Close your eyes again. Return to your garden of love. Before we focus on different areas of this garden, take a moment to ask your inner wisdom or higher power to teach you what you need to know about this garden, about love and about teaming up with your natural energy defenses to support your safety in love. If you like, you can ask your inner wisdom to adjust your beliefs and perspectives to allow you to learn more deeply. As you allow this energy of wisdom into your mind, heart and gut, into all time and no time, into your genetics and your soul, notice how your natural energy defenses support you in this learning. Notice how areas of fear or pent up emotions are soothed away by your natural energy defenses. As you ground these energies into the earth, again, see, feel or experience your natural energy defenses surrounding and supporting both your grounding cord and your connection to the earth. Allow the earth energies to do their work of synchrony and integration, and then let these synchronized energies return to you, filling you and the bubble that surrounds you.

Now get an intuitive sense about what area of love in your life needs your attention. You can ask your inner wisdom or just get a knowing in your gut. It might be love of self or body, romantic love, friendship love, giving and receiving love or some other expression or experience of love. You will find that area within your garden because each area is labeled. Notice how you feel as you get close to that part of your garden. Notice also that you might need to do some work here. It might be overgrown with weeds. Some areas might be dead. Other areas might be vibrant with health, but need some pruning or reorganizing.

Take a moment to imagine how you would like this area to look and feel and be. Also, think about what you want it to do for you. Do you want it to feed you? Perhaps you want more beauty and enjoyment or a place where you can rest and feel a deep sense of connection. You may see that parts of the garden are already changing, based on what you have imagined and discovered that you want out of love in this part of your life. Notice how different features carry symbolic meaning. Red roses might stand for romantic love, whereas vegetables might represent the love that nourishes your being. Go to any area that needs your physical labor. That might take the form of weeding or planting or adding nutrients to the soil. Let your intuition guide you about what you need. If you need tools or other things, they will appear at the entry to your garden. If you don't know what to do, ask your inner wisdom to help you know what to do.

And you can always call on your natural energy defenses to help you. Also notice that some areas simply appear with your intention. If you want a walkway, the walkway magically builds itself. If you want a stand of trees or a swath of flowers, they appear. Notice also that as this garden is being rebuilt or enhanced, earth energy is flowing through your body and inspiration energy is also showering into and through you. The more you allow this garden to organically grow in accordance with your intentions, the more enjoyable and fulfilling it is for you. As you do this, you might notice that there is an area within your own body's energy system that needs healing. If this is the case, ask your natural energy defenses to go to this part of your energy system and heal it. And ask your inner wisdom what you need to know in order for this healing to be complete. See, feel or experience this healing.

Now turn your attention back to this part of your garden of love. It may be still reorganizing, growing or changing. As it does, notice how the love and inspiration is flowing from you to the garden. Notice how good it feels to let this love flow through you. You might notice that some of the love that is flowing from your heart to this part of the garden is self-love. You might begin to notice how you love yourself in this part of your life. And notice how good it feels to let your natural energy defenses protect this part of the garden and support your growth and positive experience here. Now take a moment to open yourself to the love that is here for you in this part of your garden. You see the health, vitality and beauty here, but also let yourself feel the vibrations of love for you here. It surrounds you and draws you in. It supports and embraces you. And you can let it touch your inner being. You might feel like it is filling your heart or parts of you that are vulnerable or simply parts of you that want to be loved. Notice how safe you are with this love and how balanced and healthy it is for you. Notice how this love helps you be your real self and how easy it is to relax into it.

Now it's time to take all of these experiences of healing, growth, change, love, acceptance and safety and ground them down into the earth. Imagine that all of these experiences and energies flow through you, down through your feet, down to that place where you connect to the earth. Allow the earth energies to integrate and synchronize these experiences and energies. As you do so, you might feel as if you are changing somehow. That is fine. Just allow the earth to process these energies for you. Now allow the integrated energies to rise up into and fill your body. Let them shower up out the top of your head, filling the bubble that surrounds you.

Now it's time to return to your room and return to your chair, but before you do, let's take a moment to remember all we have done. You remember your garden of love with its different areas. You remember learning about love and choosing an area of love to enhance and learn about. You remember the area that represents this love for you and all of the changes you wanted to make. You remember putting in work and effort to make those changes, and you remember too how your natural energy defenses helped you and healed you and how the garden began to grow naturally, fueled by your love and inspiration. You remember also what it felt like to give love to this area in your life and what it felt like to receive love from this area. You remember how it touched you, its safety and your fulfillment in experiencing this love. You remember grounding all of these experiences and energies down into the earth where the earth energies made them your own, and how it felt to allow all of those integrated energies fill you and the bubble that surrounds you.

Now it's time to come back to the room and back to your chair. Feel your feet, feel your hands and fingers. Feel the breath going in and out of your lungs, and perhaps the smile on your lips. When you are ready, take a big, deep breath and open your eyes.

Follow up questions

What area of love did you focus on and what did you learn about that area of love in your life?

What does this area of your garden look like?

What symbolism did you notice and what does it mean to you?

What needed changing or healing? Do you need to change anything in your real life to support the love you want in your life? If so, what do you need to do differently?

Did this help you feel safer? Please describe.

Frequently Asked Questions

Do I need to do these meditations more than once?

Most people will have to do these meditations more than once. While we would like healing and growth to be like flipping a switch, unfortunately, it doesn't work that way. Healing and growth are more like a spiral. With every new plateau you reach, your perspective changes, and you have room for more good to flow into your life. I'm not sure that there is ever any end to the spiral. Use these meditations in ways that work for you. You may find from a new perspective, that you will discover other ways to access wisdom and growth. If you do, understand that these meditations have served their purpose, and it's time to move on. See it as a graduation.

Why the emphasis on love?

My flippant answer is that love is great, and of course we focus on love! The real answer is that most healing modalities have some reliance on love, compassion or gratitude. The energy reason for this is that love has a high frequency. While that might sound like new age gobbeldy gook, it is based on the perspective that everything in the universe is made up of energy and all of this energy is in motion, vibrating and that this energy in motion is made up of a web or system of interconnecting fields. These fields and the way they vibrate will determine how they are expressed into reality. The higher the frequency, the more complex the expression. The more complex the expression, the more rich the experience. Investigate the cutting edge philosophy that is associated with quantum mechanics, and you will see many scientists who believe that everything in the universe has some kind of consciousness, and that all of it is interconnected and that the diversity of the universe is dependent on the frequencies of the vibrations.

Are any of these things real?

This system is based on a combination of guided imagery and energy healing. The basic tenets of guided imagery say that whatever you visualize in your mind, when deeply focused, your body will take as true. Try this for yourself, relax your body and imagine that you are on the top of a skyscraper. Really get into the moment. Imagine the temperature, the scents, what you see and hear. Now imagine that you are at the edge of the roof, ready to step off into thin air. Did your heart rate go up? Did you feel fear or excitement? Did you break into a sweat? This is the body-mind connection that is the foundation of guided imagery. Your conscious mind can know that it is just a story while your subconscious lives it as truth. (FYI, I borrowed this example from Jack Canfield's program, "Self Esteem and Peak Performance).

Energy healing on the other hand, I believe, is based on reality. The reason for this belief is that I can feel life force energy flowing through my body. Also, many people find healing and growth through energy healing. I've experienced this in my own life, and I've seen it in the lives of my clients. The "story" of your energy defense system working in the ways I have described in this book is a story, but I hope that as you move through these exercises, that story will become a profound one. I hope that the story will be so impactful that you begin to experience protection, love, wisdom and goodness flowing through you. I hope this story will unlock your inner healing and protective energies. It is my hope that the story of your natural energy defenses will bring good into every corner of your life, for I believe each of us carries the potential to be protected and fueled by positive life force energy, otherwise known as love. If these stories bring you more love and goodness, more safety, wisdom and health, they will fulfill their purpose.

How does the energy of my authority (Exercise 15) work when it comes to karma?

> Although I'm not an expert in this, I do believe that unwanted things do come into life in order to teach us or help us grow. The best way to deal with things that are unwanted or painful or scary is to simply ask your inner wisdom what you need to know about it and if there is more for you to learn or do in relation to that issue. Your natural energy defenses will never impede your soul's growth, but they will help and support you along the way.

What if I have a counselor or am under psychiatric care?

> Use this book and these exercises with the guidance of your counselor or psychiatrist. They know you as an individual and know how to best use guided imagery to help and support you. This is especially true if you are suffering from post traumatic stress, depression or psychotic episodes. In the case of post traumatic stress or depression, you may need support in managing the release of emotion that results from healing. For people who suffer from psychotic episodes, you are balancing a number of factors, your treatment, perhaps medication, life stresses that exacerbate your condition and more. You will need help and support in staying grounded while doing these exercises. It is my hope that they will help you become more grounded and more empowered in your health and happiness. Don't go it alone.

What if I don't have a counselor and feel that I might need one? Should I do these exercises?

> Find a counselor and do these exercises with their help. Realsimple.com provides a great article to help readers figure out how to find a therapist at: www.realsimple.com/health/mind-mood/emotional-heal

th/how-to-find-a-therapist. Psychcentral.com offers an article with ideas if you can't afford therapy at: www.psychcentral.com/blog/what-to-do-when-you-cant-afford-therapy/. Or you can google, "crisis lines for mental health" and find resources in your area. If you are suicidal, call the National Suicide Prevention Lifeline at: 1-800-273-8255 and get help now.

Can I do these exercises instead of seeking medical care?

No.

Will doing these exercises make me safe from Covid-19?

These exercises are not meant to guarantee anything. Period. That means you still have to wear your PPE, still have to restrict your physical connection to others, and still have to take all of the precautions that a reasonable, self-loving individual would take to avoid contact with the virus. These exercises are meant to augment, support and inform your inner energy system and bring balance to your system. At the same time, the pandemic may bring opportunities for you to grow as a person and develop greater strength, courage and balance in facing situations that are stressful, uncomfortable or downright scary. Use these exercises as education for your inner being, not as a form of magic, which they are not.

Will doing these exercises make me immune from conflict?

These exercises are meant to help you to more easily meet conflict while at the same time help you make choices that lead to more safety, peace and fulfillment. Once you learn how to make boundaries in particular areas in your life, the conflict around those areas just stops appearing in your life. I've seen that over and over again in my own life. But you have to learn how to make the boundaries or deal with the situation in order to move past it. If you find that conflict is showing up in your world, try to see it as an opportunity to learn and grow in ways that help you know how to meet that conflict, resolve it or let it go.

Doing these exercises leaves me feeling cranky.

In the energy healing world, this is called a "healing crisis." While this term sounds worse than it is, its cause is doing too much too fast. It's as if you can't quite keep up with processing the energy. First of all, make sure you have the support you need. Do you need to talk to a therapist? Also, ease up a little bit. You do that by taking more time in between exercises. For example, instead of doing two exercises per day, you do one per day or week. You can also lower the intensity of the experience by imagining that you are watching the visualization on a screen rather than being immersed in what you are imagining. Finally, if you are feeling cranky or overwhelmed in doing these meditations, pair them up with Reiki sessions. Organize your schedule so that you can have a Reiki session after you do each exercise. It will help you get more out of the meditations and help you process the emotional energy so that you don't get that cranky feeling.

What if I can't visualize?

The ability to visualize is more complex than simply seeing pictures in your mind's eye. First of all, everyone visualizes differently. Some see no picture, but they feel the experience. Some people hear the words and have a sense or a knowing that their consciousness is experiencing what is being described. Some people experience all of their senses during guided meditation and the imagined experience becomes almost like watching a video. All of these ways to experience guided meditation are good and are effective.

Other people experience guided meditations in a way that is spotty, going in and out of the "experience." If this is your experience, keep practicing. It may be that you are not used to meditating and the part of the brain that focuses in this way needs to grow. Or you may have resistance in some part of your energy system that needs healing and growth.

Some people fall asleep. If you are a person who falls asleep and you are listening to audio, try speeding up the playback. The audio might be putting your brainwave activity into delta range, which leads to sleep. In the alternative, make sure you are sitting in a chair, not laying down.

If you have absolutely no ability to visualize, you may have a condition called aphantasia. This condition affects about 2% of the population. If you can't visualize at all and want to use this book, try using the cues as affirmations or mantras while you are in a meditative state. For example, with your eyes closed and body relaxed, you say to yourself, "I see myself in a place of nature....I feel the sun on my skin.....I see myself beginning to wander and I see a big castle with a spire in the distance...." I base this suggestion on comments I have read from those who have aphantasia. I can't say I know that this will work because it may take too much "work" to allow your mind to relax and focus. Try it out and send me your feedback.

Conclusion

We've come to the end of our journey of learning, healing and change. You have grown your inner resources to bring you more safety by using your inner wisdom and inner love. Before you go, I encourage you to take stock and see how far you have come. One easy way to do that is to review your answers to the follow up questions to see if your answers today would be different or if you know more now than you did at the beginning of your healing journey. Regardless, let's revisit the work you have done to view your progress.

Our first meditation introduced the concepts of your natural energy defenses and your inner wisdom. Get in touch with your inner wisdom. Notice how easy it is now and how much more you know about it. Get a feel or image of your natural energy defenses and notice how you feel as you do so. Realize how much you have learned and what it does for your ability to meet your life with confidence and a feeling of being supported.

Our second meditation expanded on the above topics and helped you understand more about your uniqueness as an energetic being. Perhaps you gained insight about your ability to hold your energetic space. Perhaps it helped you feel unconditional love flowing to you. Remember how you experienced love flowing from the earth to you and to your natural energy defenses. How do you feel about love flowing to you every minute of every day? Notice how you feel about this and how life felt before doing that meditation.

Our third meditation helped you sort out what belongs in your life and what does not. It helped you create a boundary around what is right for you. Notice how making these boundaries gives you more focus and more power or interest in the parts of your life that are yours. If you think about this boundary around your sphere of influence, how does it make you feel? Notice that the more you allow your natural energy defenses to augment the boundary with its high vibrational love energy, the more you get to allow the love to flow through you.

Our fourth meditation turned your attention to all people and things that are at the periphery of your sphere of influence. They make up the background of your life. Were you surprised that you had things to learn about your connections to the periphery of your life, your sense of global or national community. It might also relate to other kinds of community. You, as a member of these communities, have energetic relationships with them. Notice how your inner wisdom and natural energy defenses can help you navigate your experiences with these communities in easier ways.

Our fifth meditation related to people, places and things that are not necessarily a part of your personal life, but people and things that can have a strangely strong impact on you. Have you ever wondered why you care what strangers or near strangers think about you? The fourth meditation helped you get clear about those kinds of connections.

Our sixth meditation began to hone in on people and things that make up your daily life or touch your inner self or identity. Notice how much meaning is in those relationships and how much opportunity for increasing goodness or safety or wisdom or whatever is needed in this part of your life. Notice also that the changes that made a difference to you were changes in yourself, either through a shift of perception or perhaps new intentions or ways of being.

Our seventh meditation focused on the areas where energy defense based on love rather than aggression or fear really makes a difference. These are the people, places and things that help us feel like life is worthwhile and help us develop as human beings. Your ability to be safe while being real with these people is such a gift to yourself and to your loved ones. Remember what it felt like to say with your heart, "This is me." Remember what it felt like to receive a safe and loving response. It is a celebration of you, and I celebrate this along with you.

Our eighth meditation gave you new opportunities to experience your core self. Can you remember what your core self looked or felt like? This meditation helped you experience your own energy and find new ways to be safe with yourself. This kind of healing and growth can add so much to your experience of safety.

The next three meditations related to resistance. Often, our ability to confront and work with resistance makes all the difference in our ability to grow and change. The purpose of these exercises was to help you access both deeper healing and deeper connection to what guides and supports you. You also learned how to transform your relationship with your subconscious to a kind partnership, a new kind of gentleness that grows safety from the inside out.

The twelfth mediation is all about conflict, one area that does not feel safe for most of us. It gave you a new perspective and helped you listen and learn from your inner wisdom about new approaches and new techniques for conflict resolution. It allowed you to feel and know that you and your energy are different and separate from the energy of conflict. Feeling and knowing this separation gave you the objectivity to be able to resolve the conflict energy and know more.

The next meditation centered on your power. You got a chance to change your perspectives and beliefs about power and about your right and ability to use power. Your new understandings, along with your partnership with your love fueled natural energy defenses, prepared you to use your power in ways that serve your highest good and do so in ways that allow you to feel good about yourself.

The fourteenth meditation helped you find new ways to stay grounded when you interact with people who are not. It perhaps helped you see that in the past you may have given your power away or depressed your power in unsafe or unsatisfying ways to try to deal with the people around you. Remember what it felt like to accept your gifts of authority, discernment and self-love and how to use them in your life. With these gifts, you can hold your energy space, make wise decisions and treat your groundedness with the respect it deserves.

The fifteenth meditation helped you look at addictions in your life and release the pains or wounds that have chained those addictions to you. Remember the forest with its clearing and how the forest and the sunlight and your natural energy defenses supported and managed this healing. Get in touch with how much you have healed in your life. Even if there is more to resolve or more to learn, give yourself credit for having the courage and resilience to look at these deep issues and bring goodness in to make positive change.

The next two meditations had to do with health. The first one helped you feel health and to know it as it flowed throughout your system. The second one gave you new images and new experiences of infectious disease disintegrating and your cells with a security upgrade that blocks and repels all disease from all of your cells. The purpose of this meditation is to engage the placebo effect by giving your subconscious healing and positive imagery to bolster your immune function.

The final three meditations relate to sexuality, money, success, reputation and love. All of them have to do with different kinds of pleasure, joy, fulfillment and the things that drive us in our lives. Recall what you learned about pleasure. Remember how all of these things are meant to be protected by your natural energy defenses. And remember the joy and pleasure you felt in giving and receiving love once you were able to heal and allow yourself to be protected in your experience of giving and receiving love.

In reviewing all of this, I hope you see all the great things that you have done. Now that you have all of these tools, you are prepared to take on the world and do and live the things that are most meaningful for you. Be well, be safe and be happy.

About the Author

Shari Stevens is a lawyer, energy healer, teacher, guided imagery therapist, performer, nature lover and all around DYI project junkie who lives in Iowa City, Iowa. For over 20 years, Shari has helped clients overcome physical, emotional and spiritual challenges of all sorts. When she isn't writing or working with clients, you will find her in her garden, in her kayak or tinkering with a building project. You can find out more about her and other resources at: www.sharistevens.com.

Made in the USA
Monee, IL
22 January 2021

58044110R00118